THE LIBRARY OF HOLOCAUST TESTIMONIES

For Love of Life

The Library of Holocaust Testimonies

Editors: Antony Polonsky, Sir Martin Gilbert CBE,
Aubrey Newman, Raphael F. Scharf, Ben Helfgott MBE

Under the auspices of the Yad Vashem Committee of the Board of
Deputies of British Jews and the Centre for Holocaust Studies,
University of Leicester

My Lost World by Sara Rosen
From Dachau to Dunkirk by Fred Pelican
Breathe Deeply, My Son by Henry Wermuth
My Private War by Jacob Gerstenfeld-Maltiel
A Cat Called Adolf by Trude Levi
An End to Childhood by Miriam Akavia
A Child Alone by Martha Blend
The Children Accuse by Maria Hochberg-Marianska and Noe Gruss
I Light a Candle by Gena Turgel
My Heart in a Suitcase by Anne L. Fox
Memoirs from Occupied Warsaw, 1942–1945
by Helena Szereszewska
Have You Seen My Little Sister? by Janina Fischler-Martinho
Surviving the Nazis, Exile and Siberia by Edith Sekules
Out of the Ghetto by Jack Klajman with Ed Klajman
From Thessaloniki to Auschwitz and Back
by Erika Myriam Kounio Amariglio
Translated by Theresa Sundt
I Was No. 20832 at Auschwitz by Eva Tichauer
Translated by Colette Lévy and Nicki Rensten
My Child is Back! by Ursula Pawel
Wartime Experiences in Lithuania by Rivka Lozansky Bogomolnaya
Translated by Miriam Beckerman
Who Are You, Mr Grymek? by Natan Gross
Translated by William Brand
A Life Sentence of Memories by Issy Hahn, Foreword by
Theo Richmond
An Englishman at Auschwitz by Leon Greenman
For Love of Life by Leah Iglinski-Goodman
No Place to Run: A True Story by Tim Shortridge and
Michael D. Frounfelter
A Little House on Mount Carmel by Alexandre Blumstein
From Germany to England Via the Kindertransports by Peter Prager
By a Twist of History: The Three Lives of a Polish Jew by Mietek Sieradzki
The Jews of Poznań by Zbigniew Pakula
Lessons in Fear by Henryk Vogler
To Forgive ... But Not Forget by Maja Abramowitch

For Love of Life

LEAH IGLINSKI-GOODMAN

VALLENTINE MITCHELL
LONDON • PORTLAND, OR

First Published in 2002 in Great Britain by
VALLENTINE MITCHELL
Crown House, 47 Chase Side
Southgate, London N14 5BP

and in the United States of America by
VALLENTINE MITCHELL
c/o ISBS, 5824 N. E. Hassalo Street
Portland, Oregon 97213-3644

Website: http://www.vmbooks.com

British Library Cataloguing in Publication Data

Iglinski-Goodman, Leah
    For love of life. – (The library of Holocaust testimonies)
    1. Iglinski-Goodman, Leah 2. Jewish children in the holocaust –
    Belgium 3. Holocaust, Jewish (1939–1945) – Belgium – Personal
    narratives
    I. Title
    940.5′318′092

                    ISBN 0-85303-413-3
                    ISSN 1363-3759

Library of Congress Cataloging-in-Publication Data

A catalog record for this book is available from the Library of Congress

Typeset in Great Britain by FiSH Books, London WC1.
Printed in Great Britain by MPG Books Ltd, Bodmin, Cornwall

In loving memory
of my sister
Sylvia Luftman Iglinski
(1935–46)

And with hope for the future
for Michele, Robert,
and my grandchildren:
Sam, Kimberley and Billy

Contents

List of Illustrations

The Library of Holocaust Testimonies

It is greatly to the credit of Frank Cass that this series of survivors' testimonies is being published in Britain. The need for such a series has long been apparent here, where many survivors made their homes.

Since the end of the war in 1945 the terrible events of the Nazi destruction of European Jewry have cast a pall over our time. Six million Jews were murdered within a short period; the few survivors have had to carry in their memories whatever remains of the knowledge of Jewish life in more than a dozen countries, in several thousand towns, in tens of thousands of villages and in innumerable families. The precious gift of recollection has been the sole memorial for millions of people whose lives were suddenly and brutally cut off.

For many years, individual survivors have published their testimonies. But many more have been reluctant to do so, often because they could not believe that they would find a publisher for their efforts.

In my own work over the past two decades, I have been approached by many survivors who had set down their memories in writing, but who did not know how to have them published. I realized what a considerable emotional strain the writing down of such hellish memories had been. I also realized, as I read many dozens of such accounts, how important each account was, in its own way, in recounting aspects of the story that had not been told before, and adding to our understanding of the wide range of human suffering, struggle and aspiration.

With so many people and so many places involved, including many hundreds of camps, it was inevitable that the historians and students of the Holocaust should find it difficult at times to grasp the scale and range of the events.

The publication of memoirs is therefore an indispensable part of the extension of knowledge, and of public awareness of the crimes that had been committed against a whole people.

Sir Martin Gilbert
Merton College, Oxford

Foreword

It is impossible not to feel relief, in looking back through the twentieth century, that we have entered the twenty-first, and to hope that the horrors of the former can be put behind us. Unfortunately there is little possibility of that. The demarcation of time is merely an artefact devised by man to tick off the passage of events. We may go out to buy the current diary, or with some satisfaction tear from the calendar the last sheet of the month before the Millennium, but the events of the terrible twentieth century do not go away. They demand to be remembered, on the assumption that the more we do so the less likely are they to come round again.

This story is told from the experiences of Leah Iglinski-Goodman, who as a Jewish child was hidden in German-occupied Belgium during the Second World War. She describes what most impressed her through four years of concealment in a convent, and immediately afterwards.

Though there are, understandably, gaps in her recollections – as how could there not be? – she has written a vivid account of her inexplicable incarceration, with her sister and then later alone. She had no fixed notion as to how much time was passing, and such sudden separation from a large and loving family in early childhood had an effect on the rest of her life. Though her horrors are subtly related, the story is none the less instructive in how she dealt with the uncertainties and terrors of such an anguished childhood.

Though Leah was physically saved by the nuns, the imprisonment and abandonment robbed her of her childhood. At that same time, I was a sixteen-year-old working in a factory, helping to produce parts of aero-engines for Lancaster bombers, which contributed to defeat the evil regime responsible for her fate.

There must be gaps in the writer's recollections after 50

years, as I know there are in mine, but whatever these may be they serve to make what detail has survived from Iglinski-Goodman's memory that much more vivid and succinct. Though there are obviously some unanswerable questions, as to what she can remember during that life-threatening and therefore vitally formative time, we are still left with enough of a narrative to guess what they might have been.

Such a journey of rediscovery never ends, and the author of this book can live in hope that more from the past might yet be revealed. Memory is a subtle and effective way of defeating the supposed inexorability of time, and this volume shows how it can be done.

Alan Sillitoe
January 2002

Acknowledgements

First and foremost, I want to thank the creative writing group at the Holocaust Survivor Centre, Hendon: Andrew Herskovits, Martha Blend, Ester Friedman, Trude Levi, Rosa Fuhrmann, Rose Ellis, Renée Treital, Melanie Reder, Harry Ernstoff, Avram Schayfeld, Etta Lerner, Susan Ruru, for their constructive support, and Dani Jeffrey, who helped in the initial editing.

I want to express particular appreciation to the novelist Alan Sillitoe, without whose encouragement and hard work this book would not have been completed.

Uncle Joel Iglinsky is my late mother's brother. In 1936 Joel emigrated to Palestine. Later, he settled in Negba, where he and other immigrants helped cultivate what was then a desert, one of the first Kibbutz. He still lives in Kibbutz Negba, and recently celebrated his ninetieth birthday. I owe him my gratitude for giving me treasured family photographs, some of which are reproduced in this book.

Thanks are also due to the following people:

My cousin Charlie Frankfurt, for some of the historical facts related to my father's side of the family, and for the family-group photograph of himself with his parents, my Aunt Sara and Uncle Abraham.

My cousin Lyn Iglinsky, Uncle Joel's grand-daughter, for teaching me to use a computer.

Judy Hassan, director of Shalvata, for her constant support.

Rieke and Peter Nash, my cousins, for taking me to Belgium to look for the convent, and to research my family background.

My cousin Evelyne Korn, for the photographs of us in Blankenberg on the beach after the war, and of my father and me.

Rona Harding, Soti, Natasia and Jamie Demetriou, Julian

Child, Rachel Bar-Iglinsky, Anat Palenker, Dr Ruth Hill, Nitya Lacroix, Rene Inow, Simon Fremder, Nava Arieli, for their support and patience.

The staff at the Jewish Museum in Mechelen, Belgium, for providing the historical records on Deportation and the Resistance.

I have changed the names of some individuals unconnected to me by family so as to protect their privacy, but have retained those of all my relations.

1 The Cellar

I remember that first morning as if it were yesterday. I was not much more than three years old. A cold breeze swept across my face while my body shivered beneath the crisp, starched sheets. Instinctively, I knew that I was in an unfamiliar place. Gripped by fear, I was unwilling to open my eyes. I cried out, again and again: 'Mama, Mama, Sylvia, Mama.' But no one came. No one was there.

I was all alone in this dungeon place. The giant stone walls concealed frightening monsters, and the ceiling, the floor and the huge wooden door... Their threatening shape and grey colour made my body curl tight into a foetus position. I sobbed myself to sleep. When I woke up again and looked around, I thought I could see my sister.

Sylvia lay asleep on a single divan bed propped against the wall at the far side of the cellar. I had missed her at first glance, because the bedcovers were the same colour as the stone walls. It was only when I saw her pale face peeping between the covers that I realised she was there. Relieved, I leapt out of bed, ran barefoot across the cold concrete floor, and climbed in next to her.

She woke, startled, rubbed the sleep from her eyes, smiled faintly, drew me closer, and covered both our faces with the sheet. Then, ever so carefully, I pulled the sheet down from my eyes, just enough to be able to gaze at the high, grey ceiling and surrounding walls. I heard nothing, but the silence roared like thunder in my ears, jolting my body to an upright sitting position.

I had been living with my Polish-born parents and my sister Sylvia at 47 Rue Jolly, in Brussels. Shortly after my second birthday my parents separated. My mother, Sylvia and I returned to 14 Bleekery Strasser, in Antwerp: moving back into the family house with my maternal grandparents. Furriers by trade, and quite well off, they were only too happy to help our mother in every possible way.

Antwerp was densely populated by Jewish immigrants from all parts of Europe, including Poland and Russia. My grandparents worked from early morning till late into the evening, six days a week except on Shabbat.[1] Like most Jewish couples their main concern was to provide as well as they could for their family, and try to ensure that the children received a sound education. For them it was a *mitzvah*[2] to work. Money saved meant security, if not for themselves, then for the future of their five children. They wanted to save them the deprivations they themselves had experienced during their young adult lives.

In May 1940 Hitler's armies invaded Belgium, and the atmosphere in the country changed dramatically. Tension and fear swept the nation as the Nazis advanced. My father, his sister Sara, her husband Abraham and their children, Dena, Luzer and Charlie, together with thousands of people fleeing from the German army, left Brussels by train for Paris. However, the train was unable to stop there, and they went all the way to Toulouse.

For us in Antwerp, during this period, being Jewish meant that our lives were under immediate and constant threat. One day, in 1942, we came home from shopping to find the house ransacked, the entire contents tipped over or smashed, and all valuable items stolen. The french windows in the bedroom were broken and splintered glass covered the floor.

Five of us slept on mattresses among the debris, and during the night I heard soft weeping and whispering from Mama and Grandma Itta. I eventually fell asleep to the sound of their voices, feeling something momentous was about to happen.

These memories of that night are all I was left with, because the events which took place between sleeping and waking did not register in my conscious mind.

---

1 Jewish Sabbath which goes from sundown on Friday to sundown on Saturday.
2 Duty done with joy.

2

Beneath the sheets, Sylvia's small body shook like a conveyer belt, and her crying touched me to the core. Helpless and confused, my infant mind made a wish that this would turn out to be no more than a bad dream. Our wet eyes met like magnets, searching for a source of reassurance, for some truth to reveal itself: a clue, a sign of hope.

In this brief but vital moment I found comfort in the eyes of my dear, big sister, who was seven years old. Holding each other close, one of her tears fell onto the tip of my nose like a drop of warm rain and, in the emotional turmoil, her gentle voice helped to calm me.

Of the many things about Sylvia which I always remember, her patience and gentle manner are uppermost.

It was my good fortune and blessing to have her not only as a sister but as a very special friend. I buried my head into her shoulder. 'Sylvia, I don't like it here, I'm really scared. I want to go home. I want to be with Mama. Where is Mama? Is she coming?'

'Yes, *chérie*, she'll be here very soon. Last night, while you were sleeping, Mama, Grandma Itta, and Grandpa brought us on a train and tram ride, and left us here. They said we must stay for a short time, because this is the safest place for us, far away from those wicked soldiers who want to kill us.' She demonstrated what killing was by holding out her arms in front of me and shouting: 'BANG! BANG! Now you're dead! You would never see me again if you were dead and I would never see you again if I was dead.'

I playfully twisted several strands of her thick brown hair. 'Would we be like my doll Jacquie, with her broken head?'

'Yes, just like your doll.'

'I don't want soldiers to go "BANG! BANG!" We didn't do naughty things, did we? So they can't kill us, can they? Let's run away and find a soldier and say we're ever so good... well, sometimes we're naughty too, but...but...now we promise to be good always. Then he won't kill us.'

I was full of enthusiasm. It all seemed so straightforward and simple, but of course it wasn't like that at all. 'Come on Sylvia, come on!' I shouted, grasping her hand in an attempt to get her off the bed. 'Get up, let's go!'

She wouldn't move, pulled away from my grip and

fidgeted nervously with the corner of the sheet, twisting it around her wrist like a bandage. I was frustrated more than angry because she wasn't prepared to escape. To show how determined I was, even ready to go alone if necessary, I stormed across the concrete floor and climbed the half dozen high stone steps. Facing the enormous wooden door on tiptoe, I was convinced that if I stretched my arm high enough I could reach the handle and we could both get away.

After several unsuccessful attempts I became enraged, and, in sheer frustration, banged my fists, kicked the door and screamed as loudly as I could until, exasperated by the ordeal, I threw myself on the floor.

The concrete under my face and body was as cold as ice. Feeling like a trapped animal I clawed frantically at the ground in the hope that it would open up. I was suffocating, feeling as if buried alive in a huge tomb.

I felt Sylvia's warm breath on my cheek as she crouched on the concrete and took me in her arms. 'Even if we could escape,' she whispered, 'the soldiers wouldn't believe us. Because there's this man called Hitler who is in charge of the German army and he hates the Jews. His orders are to kill all of them, including children like us. So you see, we have to hide, that's why we're here. Mama told me this and lots more last night before she kissed us goodbye. She said that here we have a chance to be saved, because this is a house of God.'

'How long do we have to stay?'

Sylvia looked worried. A frown appeared on her forehead and her large oval eyes, dark as coal, were uncertain. 'I don't know, but I promise it won't be long, because Mama said she'll be back very, very soon. So you see, Leah, that's the reason we mustn't run away. What do you imagine Mama would feel and think if she came and found us gone?'

'She would cry and worry, but is she really coming soon?'

'Yes, yes,' Sylvia smiled. I was overjoyed. Soon meant NOW! What did I understand about minutes, tomorrow, next week, a month, a year? It meant nothing. I simply held on to the vision that Mama was coming to take us home again, far away from this place, and nothing else mattered. I was so happy that I burst into a song about Mama, making up the lyrics as I went along. We jumped on the wooden table in the middle of the cellar as though it were a stage, dancing and lifting our nighties like chorus girls. For a while I forgot where I was, as if transported to another place, dancing on the kitchen table at home. I stopped suddenly, as a thought struck me.

'Why isn't Mama hiding with us?' I asked Sylvia, as she spun around.

'Because the nuns will only take children.' She flapped her arms, pretending to be a bird about to fly away.

'Where are the other children?'

'There aren't any. We are the only ones here.'

'Why wouldn't they take grown-ups?'

'I don't know why,' Sylvia replied irritably.

'What will happen to Mama if the soldiers find her? Will they kill her?'

'Don't say that! She isn't going to get caught and nothing's going to happen to her.' She was upset by my question. We sat on the edge of the table swinging our legs to and fro.

After a long silence I said: 'Talk to me, Sylvia.'

'I'm sorry, *chérie*, I shouldn't shout at you and then sulk. You're such a little baby. I won't do it again.' We hugged each other and, feeling hungry and cold, slipped back into bed.

The loud ringing of church bells startled me out of my sleep. Sylvia stirred and groaned under the blankets. I counted four, five, and on the sixth stroke the tolling stopped. I tapped Sylvia on the arm. Her voice was faint and muffled. 'What is it, *chérie*?'

'The noise of the bells is in my head.'

'Mine, too. Next time it happens let's shake our heads and then swallow hard, that should help.'

It didn't make the slightest difference. The vibration of the bells every hour came through the stone walls and dominated my whole being. When I complained, Sylvia said: 'Well, let's put our fingers in our ears and keep our eyes shut tight. That might stop the noise getting into our bodies.'

'That's a good idea. I don't know what I'd do without you Sylvia.'

She gave that special smile which lightened up her face. 'And I don't know what I'd do without you, little sister 'cos I love you more than the whole world.' In my joy and enthusiasm, I rolled out of bed and teasingly threw the pillows at her.

'Why, you little rascal!' She make a beeline for me, and chased me around the cellar as I ducked and dived to avoid being caught. Finally she picked me up and threw me onto the bed where I bounced like a ball. She began to tickle me. 'Please, no more tickling!' I screamed. But the more I pleaded and giggled the more she went on.

'I hate you!' I said, desperately trying to control myself. 'I could even die from too much laughing!'

'Then how about making a promise?'

'Yes, yes, anything. Just stop! What shall I promise?'

'Not to hit me on my head again, not even with a pillow. You don't realise how tender my head is. Just the weight of the pillow hurts it. It's true.'

I could tell she was in pain by the way she clutched her head with both hands, I had forgotten she'd often complained to Mama about headaches. 'I won't do it again, I promise.'

A key turned on the other side of the wooden door, and two bolts slid back, click-clack. The heavy door opened in slow motion, squeaking all the while, until a figure appeared in the doorway, dressed in a long robe, a tray in both hands. The woman stood motionless for several seconds. A stiff headdress covered most of her forehead, the rest of her head and shoulders were hidden under a loose veil.

Sylvia and I looked at each other in disbelief, as if she had come from another planet. She looked so weird but, judging from the expression on her face, she probably thought the same about us.

'Girls, come and sit on the bench.' She placed the tray on the rectangular table. 'Here's your breakfast.'

'*Bonjour*,' we replied. 'Why do you wear a long dress, and that funny thing on your head? Does it hurt?'

'It looks ever so silly,' I said.

'What an inquisitive child you are. Even if I were to explain it to you, I doubt that you'd understand.'

'*Si, si*, we would, wouldn't we Sylvia?'

The strange woman stood at the edge of the table, her hands clasped below her stomach.

'Have you got hair under that thing?' I stepped on to the bench in an attempt to lift the veil and see for myself.

She backed away, turned her head to one side, and with raised eyebrows peered over the spectacles perched on the edge of her uptilted nose. 'Now, that's quite enough questions. And get down from the bench at once.'

'No! Why should I? I'm not doing anything wrong.'

The stranger took a deep breath, sighed, adjusted her glasses, then left us alone again in the cellar. She came back in what seemed like a few minutes, and stood with her hands on her hips: 'Why haven't you touched your breakfast?'

'I don't want to sound rude or anything, but we don't like it, it's really awful!' Sylvia scooped a heap of porridge onto the spoon and held it high above her head. She turned the spoon on its side. 'Look at it! It's so thick and lumpy it won't even come off the spoon. The sight of it makes me feel sick. I just can't eat it!'

The woman's fingers moved slowly up and down her hips as if on piano keys. Sylvia pushed the metal bowl so that it slid down the table. 'Could we please have an egg instead?'

'This is all you're going to get,' said the stranger, 'and if you don't eat it, there'll be nothing else till lunch-time. So you'd better get used to what you're given. I suggest you start immediately. The sooner the better is what I say. As far as eggs are concerned, it's absolutely out of the question. So what will it be? Either you eat what's in front of you, or you go hungry.'

There was no point saying anything, so we kept quiet, Sylvia on the verge of tears.

'You'd better make your mind up quickly. I haven't time to stand around all day,' she said.

Sylvia shrugged her shoulders and I did the same.

'Very well, I'll leave you to your own devices.' She paused for a moment then, pointing a finger directly at Sylvia, went on: 'You'd better get yourself and your sister dressed.' With her shoulders back and head held high, she left the cellar.

As the morning wore on we became very hungry and, with only one of two options, ate the cold porridge, scraping the bowls like scavengers.

'She's right, we'll eat anything, whether we like it or not. Look how we're stuffing ourselves with this gunge, just to stop our bellies from feeling empty. Wait till Mama gets to hear about this...' Sylvia suddenly covered her mouth with her hand, leapt from the table, and was sick all over the floor and on her clothes. There was no water in the cellar so it was difficult to clean up the mess, but we did what we could, which was to scoop it up with a spoon and put it back into the bowl.

For the rest of the day nothing happened. We saw no one, except the stranger, who came with lunch and, just before bedtime, with bread thinly spread with jam, and mugs of watery milk.

We eventually learned that her name was Sister Marie-Jeanne, and that we were in a convent. A young novice brought in two buckets, one filled with water for washing our faces and bodies and cleaning our teeth. The second bucket for body functions. Although the contents of the bucket were disposed of by the novice on a regular basis, the foul, offensive stench was always there.

Sister Marie-Jeanne came back when we were in our nightdresses, and told us to kneel at the edge of the bed. She gave us each a rosary, and made us repeat the evening prayer after her.

2   The Convent

A daily routine was established by Sister Marie-Jeanne. She was in her early thirties and of medium build, with the impervious solid body of an iceberg. The headdress emphasised her round face and fair complexion, and blue unyielding eyes. On the right side of her chin was a dark mole, from which came several long spiky hairs. One morning (it could have been soon after we arrived or many weeks later, I don't remember) she said in her high-pitched voice: 'Come along, girls! Follow me.'

'Yes,' Sylvia replied. We were overjoyed, for it was the first time since our arrival that we were leaving the cellar. We burst into fits of laughter, and hugged one another tight. With hands firmly gripped together, we ran for our lives through the open door. Sister Marie-Jeanne walked several paces ahead through a long, narrow, black and white tiled corridor. I felt elated that there was to be no more hiding in a cold cellar, no more being behind locks and bolts. We were on our way home.

'Where are we going, Sylvia?' I whispered.

'I don't know. Maybe Mama's come for us.'

'Yes, yes, that's what I think,' I squeaked with excitement.

'Shh,' said Sister Marie-Jeanne, 'There must be no talking along the corridor.' It was odd that the silence made time pass so slowly, and I wondered how much further we had to walk before seeing Mama. The thought of being back with her, and Grandma Itta, and the chickens, made me smile up at Sylvia. Such thoughts were diverted as we entered a strange place, which I was later to know as a chapel.

'This is how Christ our Saviour died when some of his followers betrayed him,' said Sister Marie-Jeanne.

I remember how I shuddered. My body stiffened in disbelief and shock as I stared at the blood-stained figure, larger than life, inside the dome above the altar. The statue of

Jesus together with the smell of incense, so overwhelmed me that I lost my balance. I gripped Sylvia's hand even tighter. 'So this is what death looks like. Someone could die...like this?'

A sudden cold, tingling sensation swept from top to bottom of my spine, and I couldn't help but wonder: 'What if Mama isn't here? What if she's been caught by the Germans? Would they kill her in the same way as Christ?' The sight of the bloody corpse on the cross made death much more frightening and final. It was nothing like my doll's broken head. Nothing like it at all! Suddenly I was in the middle of a hurricane, the chapel spinning around, faster and faster. Then, as mysteriously as it had begun, everything stopped and went blank.

Sylvia and Sister Marie-Jeanne were looking down at me; and I heard Sylvia's concerned voice: '*O ma petite chérie*. Are you all right? You fainted.'

'Yes I'm OK. I feel a little sick.'

'Did you hurt yourself?'

'No, but I'm cold.'

'Your sister looks better now. Stay here with her until she is steady on her feet, then come and join me. I shall be sitting over there.' Sister Marie-Jeanne pointed towards the empty seats in the chapel.

'Come,' Sylvia said, 'we must get the colour back into your cheeks.' She gently rubbed my face with her hands. 'You look like a ghost.'

As I recovered, Sylvia's words struck me as amusing. Playing ghost together was always fun. And I wanted to play it here, by the altar. I stretched out my arms, rolled my eyes as far back as they could go so that only the whites showed, then ever so quietly so that the nun wouldn't hear, I made some hideous noises, 'Oooo, oooo', as I circled around her, playing ghost. Sister Marie-Jeanne sat on a wooden bench several rows from the altar, turning the pages of the Holy Book with considerable speed and concentration.

I whispered: 'I want to tell God something. Can I Sylvia?'

'Of course. You can tell God anything you want.'

'Anything?' I was surprised.

'Yes, *chérie*.' She smiled reassuringly. 'Would you like to ask something now?'

'Shall I? Here?' I whispered, and glanced over my shoulder to see if Sister Marie-Jeanne was listening. Luckily, she was engrossed in the Holy Book. In my child's mind I wondered whether this was the right place to talk to God. After all, wasn't the God here a different God to the one Mama, Grandma Itta and Grandpa prayed to? 'Will this God listen to me?'

'Of course He will.'

I stood in front of the altar, and closed my eyes:

'Hello God, my name is Leah. Will you please not let my Mama die? Amen.'

I expected him to answer, because Grandma Itta had once said that though it was possible to hear the voice of God, only those who are sincere would understand his words. I was sure I heard a voice, but it wasn't as Grandma Itta had described. When the voice came to me again I realised as quick as lightning that it wasn't the voice of God at all.

'What's that I hear?' Sister Marie-Jeanne called out from her seat. 'Nonsense child! Your mother isn't going to die. She'll come back for the two of you.' She got up and, clutching the Holy Book to her bosom, came to the centre of the aisle, 'I want both of you down here at once!'

This frightened us so much that we jumped at her command. Walking hand in hand, Sylvia and I signalled to each other by the language of touch, as Sister Marie-Jeanne went on with absolute conviction: 'If you had faith in our Lord Jesus Christ you would know that He is keeping your mother safe.'

'How do you know?' I screamed. But Sylvia intervened before I could say another word.

'You're not with her,' she said to the nun, 'you can't see what's happening out there. Don't think you know it all, I know the Germans are killing all the Jewish people, because my mother explained it to me. And I know that if they find her, they'll kill her, because she's Jewish. So what can God or your Jesus Christ do to stop it? Nothing! Nothing at all! I know that, even though I'm only seven. You think because I'm so young I can't understand anything? We're not fools, so stop treating us as if we were.'

I held on to Sylvia's arm as if my life depended on it and, to

11

my surprise, Sister Marie-Jeanne was too astonished to respond, though if looks could...well! I was proud at the way my big sister had spoken, for it wasn't in her nature to be assertive. I'd certainly never seen her like this before. But at the same time, I was upset at what she'd said.

"Is Mama going to die? Is she? Is she? You told me she wouldn't, that she'd be coming to take us home.'

'I know, I'm sorry. Don't cry Leah. I had hoped that she would come today but, she hasn't. I don't mean that she WILL DIE! I'm just saying if she is caught by the German soldiers then...But Mama is very clever. She'll have found a wonderful hiding-place where no one will think of looking. So don't let's talk about it anymore, *chérie*, OK?'

Sister Marie-Jeanne tried to take our hands, but Sylvia put her arm around my shoulder, her body shaking uncontrollably. 'I don't want to hold your hand,' I shouted at the nun, swinging my arms behind my back to avoid contact.

Sylvia nudged my shoulder. 'You better do it,' she whispered.

'But I don't like her.'

'I don't either. But we're in enough trouble, and she could make our lives a lot worse.'

I didn't want things to be difficult, but at the same time couldn't see why I had to hold Sister Marie-Jeanne's hand, something I only did among family and friends.

Sister Marie-Jeanne led the way down the aisle, through swing-doors that took us along a dimly lit hall, and into a small room. The ceiling and walls were covered with red embossed wallpaper. Six carved oak chairs stood around an oval oak table which almost filled the room. Before each seat was what I later recognised as a gold-leaf Bible. This was the room in which two hours of religious education would take place daily from now on. I would sit gazing through the bay-windows overlooking a small part of the courtyard. Concentration was all but impossible, and besides, I had many things to think about, religion not being part of my day-dreams.

The route back to the cellar led through the courtyard, the open space our only opportunity to breathe fresh air. On a small patch of grass stood a white stone sculpture of the

Virgin Mary and child Jesus. Nearby were several wooden benches surrounded by troughs of flowers and foliage. Occasionally we saw other nuns on their leisurely stroll around the grounds.

Back in the cellar Sylvia and I kept ourselves occupied as well as we could. We were often cold, and to keep warm covered our heads and shoulders with the blankets from the bed as we played.

Jacquie, my black fabric doll, had only a few strands of woollen hair left. One mother-of-pearl button eye hung by a frail piece of thread several centimetres below its socket, and her beautiful cushioned hands and feet, soft as silken mittens, had I suppose long been a substitute for mother's breasts. Despite her shabby appearance, Jacquie had been my favourite doll before coming to the convent.

Tootsy, Sylvia's porcelain pride and joy, was kept in tip-top condition. Her eyelids opened and shut, and when the cord on her back was pulled, she said, 'mama, papa'. We took it in turns to dress her in a variety of clothes which Grandma Itta had hand-sewn from delicate silk and lace fabrics, down to the smallest item of underwear. Sometimes I would take both dolls to the far corner of the cellar, where I had created a make-believe world of my own.

We had no other toys, nor any books, pencils or paper, so had to made up games as we went along. We camouflaged the surface of the wooden table with sheets from our beds, which hung to the ground like ruched curtains. Inside this tent we spread blankets and pillows across the concrete floor, the pale, off-white sheets reflecting a soft light in the enclosed space, and keeping the grey surrounding walls out of sight.

We played at being mothers, pretending to cook familiar dishes such as chicken soup, *kreplech*, egg-noodles, chopped liver, almond cakes, apple strudel... The list was endless. Our appetite grew out of all proportion, by talking and remembering those wonderful smells that used to seep from the steaming pots and pans on top of Grandma Itta's black coal oven. Oh, how we yearned for a mouthful of home-cooking!

On one occasion the table and bench were transformed into a slide, and when Sister Marie-Jeanne set eyes on it I was hanging upside down in mid-air, Sylvia holding my ankles. She moved briskly towards us. 'Let go at once! What do you girls think this place is? A playground? It's an outrage! You're impossible creatures!'

'But it's only a bit of fun. We're not going to break it,' Sylvia explained, 'It's wood, look.' She slapped the bench with the palm of her hand. 'Please say we can play with it.'

Her plea was in vain. Sister Marie-Jeanne was in no mood to give in. She hovered around, then began replacing the wooden table and bench in the middle of the room, ignoring Sylvia, who tried to help, and talking incoherent mumbo-jumbo to herself. In an attempt to get our own back we poked our tongues out and made hideous faces behind her back.

In the following weeks we worked out the safe times to play our games. Generally, it was after lunch, when we were left on our own for long periods. Otherwise it was after bedtime.

A seat I favoured most for meals was that opposite the stained glass window set high in one of the cellar walls. Sylvia liked it too, but let me have it so that we could face each other.

The window was painted with delicate figures of cherubs, animals and plants in rich primary colours. Part of the panel was damaged, just enough for us to see a small patch of sky. A tip of the branch from a nearby tree, covered with green and pink buds, swayed gently in the breeze.

The midday meals consisted mainly of white rice or potatoes, presented in a variety of ways, either boiled, baked, or dry-mashed. The latter was more usual, with or without a slice of bread, which, if we were fortunate enough to receive one, was usually stale. I know that there are gaps in my recollections. After more than fifty years, I am still tormented by what I might have witnessed during my years in hiding to cause my mind to shut down and wipe out so much.

Every day was the same. The weeks, the months, the years. Every morning came with hope. Anticipating Mama's arrival kept Sylvia and me cheerful throughout most of the day. At nightfall, long after we had repeated the evening prayer with Sister Marie-Jeannne, Sylvia and I were uncertain again. Another day had passed ... without Mama!

Restless and unable to sleep, Sylvia sat on the bed with her back to the wall, rocking endlessly, while I, in my make-believe world, sat in the corner at the far end of the cellar, talking with our dolls, as if they were my children, explaining that one day all four of us would run away from the convent.

Exhausted, I finally lay down and went to sleep cuddling both the dolls and my sister. My only comfort was that Sylvia and I were together.

When our clothes had to be changed, having become too tight and ill-fitting, Sister Marie-Jeanne gave us new ones, although these were actually old clothes invariably in a shabby condition.

We were given underwear, dresses, jumpers, socks and shoes, everything except the underwear being second-hand. The jumpers were darned at the elbows; while the dress with large patchwork stitching on the front pocket was too big and too long, and the dark, grey, tweed fabric irritated my skin. I loathed having to wear such things.

It was obvious to Sylvia, though not to me, that we had grown. This, together with our hair being cut short several times, indicated to Sylvia that we had now been in hiding for some considerable time. For precisely how long, it was impossible for us to know. When Sylvia asked Sister Marie-Jeanne what month of the year it was, and how long had we been in the convent, she was ignored.

One day, as we made our way to the chapel, I couldn't help mimicking Sister Marie-Jeanne's body movements. We tried to contain our giggling, but I lost control and, in a panic to muffle the sound, Sylvia took the hem of my dress and stuffed it in my mouth. She was a few seconds too late, because Sister Marie-Jeanne stopped in her tracks and looked sternly over her shoulders. She wasn't the slightest bit amused. On the contrary, I had broken the code of silence. And, seeing a finger pressed firmly to her lips, I fully understood that there was no choice but to obey the order being given. I took a deep breath through my nose, opened my jaw even wider, and exhaled.

The hem of the dress parachuted out of my mouth. Wet and crinkled, it clung to my calves.

Back in the cellar, Sister Marie-Jeanne said, 'The next time you step out of line and disobey the rules and regulations, I'll send you to Mother Superior, and what she might do, I promise you will not find at all amusing. Am I making myself clear, and do you both understand the seriousness of your conduct?'

'Yes,' we replied, not really able to comprehend why she was making such fuss over a simple prank.

'I bet God has a sense of humour, and if he'd been watching he would have had a jolly good laugh.'

Sylvia tried to lighten the tension but, whatever her reasons, the remark didn't soften Sister Marie-Jeanne's attitude. If anything it made it worse.

'That's quite enough of that kind of talk! You may not mock God in my presence. Where is your respect for the Almighty? And were you never taught not to answer back to your elders? It's quite vulgar and rude for children to answer back the way both of you do. It will not be allowed to continue. Certainly not while you remain here. You will stop talking immediately!' Sylvia was about to say something but Sister Marie-Jeanne interrupted her.

'Today the two of you will scrub every inch of this floor, until there isn't a speck of dirt left. Make sure you do it thoroughly, because I'll be back to inspect it. Don't miss a spot anywhere,' she emphasised.

Minutes later, a young novice brought in two buckets, with brushes floating on the water, and a mop held tight under her arm. She placed these items to one side of the cellar, and left us to get on with the scrubbing. How long it took from start to finish I'll never know, but the cellar was vast to us, and we seemed to be on all fours, dipping into dirty water, for hours on end.

From then on, being the child I was, I could see nothing likeable in Sister Marie-Jeanne. After we had scrubbed the cellar on perhaps half a dozen occasions we realised quite by chance that pouring water directly onto the floor from the bucket was a much easier method. The bundle of coarse yarn at the base of the wooden stick mopped the stone surface clean in half the time.

'Which of you is bathing first this time?' Sister Marie-Jeanne asked, as she entered the cellar later that day, with the novice carrying two buckets of water. Her eyes narrowed, appearing half-closed as they scanned the floor.

'Me,' I replied, stripping my clothes off and leaving a scattered trail on the ground. The novice quietly went about her work, and when she finished carrying in the portable bath tub and buckets of warm water, I ran naked across the cellar to the other side. Leaping as high as I could, I plunged into the tub.

Immediately after Sister Marie-Jeanne and the novice left the cellar, Sylvia knelt at the foot of the tub, folded a towel and placed it under her knees. 'Do you remember,' she asked, gently rubbing the soap over my back, 'the time the family went on holiday together to Blankenberg?'

I hesitated. 'Yes...No.'

'You know, when we stayed in a big barn-house.'

'I don't remember all of it.'

'In front of the barn-house', she went on, 'was a big courtyard, paved with cobblestones. In between the cobbles, wild flowers grew surrounded by mounds of green fur moss. Stray cats and dogs used to come into the courtyard because the old iron gate wouldn't close. And the cats' wailing in the night only stopped when someone sprayed water over them.'

'Tell me, who came on holiday with us?'

'Let me see,' she twirled the square cake of soap several times in her hands, then gave it to me to hold. She made a circle with her thumb and first finger and breathed out gently, blowing two or more times on the moist circle. But the bubbles never came. Talk about everyone in the family came tumbling out: 'There was Auntie Sara,' she said, 'Papa's older sister. She's quite fat and wears her black hair tied back in a bun. Mama thought Sara looked Mongolian in comparison to the rest of the family.'

'What's Mongolian?'

'I'll explain it another day,' Sylvia said.

'Auntie Sara used to say that Charles and Dena were the best-behaved, most polite and intelligent children in the family. Sara insisted it had nothing to do with the fact that they were her children. Mama thought I also had above average intelligence for someone my age. Anyway, Charlie, being the oldest boy cousin, eight, maybe nine years old, was sometimes asked to babysit. While he read to us, I imagined combing his thick black wavy hair until he had finished reading the story, which usually ended too soon for me.' Sylvia embraced her own body, her cheeks turning bright red. 'I want to marry him when I'm grown up,' she giggled.

'His sister Dena and I once brought home a tiny baby bird. We found it under a tree by the pavement on our way from the beach. One of its wings had been damaged. We covered the bottom of a box with grass and put the little bird in. I kept it by the side of my bed and fed it every day with bits of chicken. We filled a saucer with water just in case the bird was thirsty while I was asleep or at the beach. Then one day, its wing having got better, the small bird flew away. Dena's fifteen, and with her olive skin she became quickly chocolate-coloured in the sun. The boys on the beach got friendly with her and soon we were playing together seeing who could jump the furthest from the cliff onto the sand.'

'Abraham, Charles and Dena's father is a little man who keeps to himself a lot of the time. He is very soft spoken. Abraham's eyes are kind.'

'Uncle Jack's a bit younger than Papa. Broader and taller. Not by much. You can tell they are brothers, because they look alike. They used to sit for hours around the dining table designing men's suits and women's dresses, and cutting them out on to large sheets of brown paper. It's what he does for his living.'

'Did he make clothes for Mama and us?'

'We were too small. But he made Mama lovely skirts and coats. I missed Papa when we moved away.'

'Why did we move?' I asked.

Sylvia paused and shrugged her shoulders. 'I'm not sure. Maybe because they always argued with one another. One day, Mama just said that we were leaving, and so we moved in with Grandma Itta and Grandpa.'

'Didn't we always live with Grandma Itta? 'Cos I don't remember living with Papa.'

'Don't you? You remember him visiting us?'

'No.'

'Maybe you were with Charlie, or with one of our aunts when Papa came round.'

This was the first and the last time, Sylvia spoke about Papa.

'Paula, Jack's wife, is a shy lady. She was always busy. Knitting, darning socks, preparing food, shopping. Paula's face glows as if she polishes it. She wears no make-up except a little pale lipstick. In this way she's different from our other aunts. She was pregnant with her first child, and all the family was excited about the arrival of another baby. She never ate much, and Uncle Jack worried about her appetite.'

'Papa's second favourite sister, after Sara, is Aunt Clara. Now Clara never stops talking. I remember she had rims around her eyes, which were red and sore. And her feet and ankles swelled in the heat so that sometimes she couldn't get them into a pair of sandals.'

'Aunt Clara's husband, Simon, came from Argentina. He has ginger hair, thin and balding at the crown. His small puffy eyes are bright blue. His pale complexion is covered in freckles. Simon is short, fat, quick-tempered and loud but, he made us laugh a lot. His diamond business in Antwerp made him rich.'

'Evelyn, their daughter, is about the same age as you. Maybe she's a year younger. She's as pretty as a doll with her black hair, and big brown eyes.'

'Albert, her blond, blue-eyed baby brother is gorgeous.'

'We hired bicycle carts and raced along the wide promenade, then played outdoor table tennis and Diabolo, which brought crowds of people who stood gaping curiously at the game.'

'Just a minute though,' she said. 'There was a red-haired boy on holiday with us too. What was his name? Now I remember. It was Freddie. That's it! A friend of the family was hoping to adopt him. I wonder what has happened to him. Of course, I nearly forgot about Aunt Gucia.'

'Who is Aunt Gucia?' I wanted to know.

'*Chérie*, Gucia is Mama's sister. She is Fanny, Sara and Yosi's Mama. Fanny lives with a foster family but I don't know why.'

'*Ah ... mais oui, c'est vrai!* But you mean Aunt Guciale Shaina Golda!'

'Yes.' Sylvia chuckled under her breath, 'That's what I said. Isn't it? Gucia, and Guciale Shaina Golda, it's the same.'

'No no,' I insisted, shaking my head.

'Well, let's see how many we were on holiday.' She held her

fingers in the air and I did the same.

'Nineteen... twenty... twenty-one.'

'That many!' I was surprised and happy. '*Ooh là là!*'

'The beach in Blankenberg,' Sylvia continued, 'stretched for miles. Like a blanket of golden sand. And far away, it seemed as if the sky and the sea were joined together. In the sunlight millions of tiny diamond-shaped lights twinkled on the surface of the sea.'

'Standing knee-deep in the crystal clear water with my fishing net, I saw hundreds of small sardines swimming in circles, in and out of the reeds. Near the rocks, large bunches of seaweed came in frightening shapes. Now and then shrimps, mussels and starfish swam up from the bottom of the sea. And you, *chérie*, you sat playing with your bucket and spade. When the fishing net was full, I emptied it next to you. You picked up one shellfish at a time. And, after having inspected it from every angle, you placed it carefully in the bucket. Sometimes a small wave knocked the bucket down, washing some of the fish back into the sea and burying a few in the sand.'

'What else did we do?' I asked.

'When you thought no one was watching you were off, quick as lightning, crawling at the edge of the waves.'

I laughed.

'It wasn't funny!' She tried to hide her smile. 'It was a miracle you didn't drown. We got some funny looks from people sitting near us, especially when Mama fetched you back to sit with her and the family. All you did was scream and cry. God knows what people thought. A little bit later one of us took you back to the sea and let you paddle. That quietened you down.' Sylvia's tone changed. As she took my hand, helping me out of the tin tub: 'Hey, *chérie*, isn't it about time I get to have a bath too?'

Her stories helped to pass the days more easily, by taking me back to the time when life had been normal. A chicken roaming around the house had been a familiar sight, as was seeing their feathers plucked in preparation for the Sabbath meal.

Grandma Itta, a short stout woman with a bossy nature, busied herself in a room making fur coats and jackets during the summer and autumn, and fur hats the rest of the year, ancient Yiddish songs echoing through our home.

I can still smell the cheese-cakes, apple, cinnamon and currant strudel, coconut and almonds baking in the cast-iron stove. I can still hear the stirring of food in earthenware pots and pans, cups rattling on to saucers, plates and cutlery tinkling under running water. I can remember the table being laid on a clean hand-embroidered tablecloth.

I visualised Aunt Clara with both hands on her hips, standing in the hallway outside the kitchen door, facing the open street door. She would shout, '*Kinderleh*,[1] come in right away. And *essen*.'[2] Like the rest of the family, she spoke in a mixture of Yiddish, Polish and French, her words carrying more weight than those of the entire family put together. All, that is, with the exception of Simon, her husband.

We would pile into the house one after the other, like a herd of baby elephants, each trying hard to overtake through the narrow entrance and along the hall. Whoever managed to reach the table first would sneer at the rest, his or her hand fingering the largest piece of sliced cake. 'That's not fair!' the others complained.

'Don't touch!' Aunt Clara shrieked, panic in her voice, palms pressed to her flushed pink cheeks. 'Go, go! Wash the *shmutsic*[3] *handleh*[4]...NOW!'

She wiped the perspiration off her face and neck with the hem of her apron, tied half-way between her waist and stomach. When we returned to the kitchen with clean hands and faces, she smiled warmly.

The cellar door opened and Sister Marie-Jeanne's unexpected appearance brought me back into the stark reality of our cell.

'What is the meaning of this? I want you out of the tub immediately!' she ordered Sylvia, in her now all-too-familiar tone.

---

1 Children.
2 eat.
3 dirty.
4 little hands.

3 Leah Alone

One morning, after breakfast, Sister Marie-Jeanne said Sylvia wasn't to go to the religious education class for that day. This being unusual, we asked why, 'You'll know soon enough!' she said. At first I refused to go to the class without Sylvia, though in the end I had no choice but to do as I was told.

On the way back Sister Marie-Jeanne and the novice turned in a different direction from the normal route. We entered a circular hall with a high domed ceiling, and a black and white mosaic tiled floor. That part of the convent had been unknown to me and, being naturally curious, I wanted to know where we were going. However, Sister Marie-Jeanne and the novice talked only Flemish, which I didn't understand, so not wanting to interrupt and appear rude, I decided to keep quiet.

We stopped in front of white double doors, affixed to which were two round brass handles that I fondled admiringly, intrigued by my distorted reflection. A close-up of my face looked bizarre, the shape strange, and two or three times its normal size. Clenching my teeth, I gave a false smile, then pulled at the corner of my eyes till they became two thin slits. My amusement came to an abrupt end when Sister Marie-Jeanne, without further explanation, swung the doors open, tapped me on the shoulder, and nudged me into the room. 'In you go!'

My first impression was of the room's immense size; then I noticed the luxurious wall-to-wall carpeting and the Eastern-style rug covering a large part of the floor.

'Come here, where I can talk to you. I'm the Mother Superior,' said the figure sitting in a leather chair behind a desk at the far side of the room. Her shoulders were stooped and her head leaned over a pile of papers.

As soon as I reached her desk she came straight to the point and matter-of-factly announced that the war had ended two weeks ago. My immediate reaction was sheer excitement, and

I clapped my hands again and again, shouting: 'Bravo bravo!' But the Mother Superior did not react. She hadn't as much as looked at me, which led me to wonder whether I had heard and understood correctly. As she went on and on talking about things which meant nothing to me, I decided to pay more attention, and heard her say that Germany had surrendered unconditionally.

I had never been so happy and excited in my life as at that moment. I was preoccupied with thoughts of being reunited with Mama, and had a strong impulse to rush out of the office and share the wonderful news with Sylvia. I knew, however, that I couldn't just walk out, nor was I given the appropriate cue to say what was on my mind, nor any reason to suspect that a few seconds later my fate would take a new direction.

While focusing on the papers before her, the Mother Superior said in a much quieter voice, 'Do you realise you have both been here for three years? It was longer than I had anticipated.'

'How long is that? How many days is three years?' I held up my fingers in front of her.

'My goodness! It's considerably more than ten fingers, my child.'

'Is it as many as all my fingers and all my toes, and Sylvia's put together? Because that's how Sylvia taught me to count. They make forty. That's a lot, isn't it!' I said, assuring the Mother Superior that forty was a very large number indeed.

'My child, there are three hundred and sixty-five days in the year. Multiplied by three, it makes one thousand and ninety-five days. That is the length of time that you have both been here.'

The Mother Superior's tone of voice embarrassed me. I felt stupid. Protesting, I shouted: 'How am I supposed to know this? Sister Marie-Jeanne never tells us nor shows us anything!'

Having no concept of time, it seemed I had been separated from Mama all my life.

'Due to unforeseen circumstances, I am regrettably no longer in a position to keep Sylvia in the convent. New arrangements have been made for your sister. She left us an hour ago.'

While I had been attending religious class, someone had taken Sylvia away. The Mother Superior's words echoed in my head. They came and faded...my tongue and lips were dry and felt like sandpaper.

'Gone? Without me? Don't say that. Don't take her away from me. Please!'

'My child, you are six years old. Try to understand that our keeping you here has been, and continues to be in your best interest. Sylvia will be taken care of. She is older than you and must go to school. She will be all right.'

I remember the feeling to this day. It's true that I didn't understand, but something within me wanted to know why Sylvia had gone. I was too shocked to speak, could only think of the fact that we hadn't even said goodbye.

Eventually I returned to the cellar, though cannot recall how, or who took me there, only realising later that from now on I was really alone. I was lethargic for days, maybe for weeks, or perhaps even longer, I can't even now be sure how long my despair lasted.

Spring 1945

Too long the plight, too weak to fight,
I let out a shrieking cry
...Mama...Mama...help me...help me...
But no one hears my plea
No one comes to rescue me.

Buried beneath the bedclothes, accompanied by fear
Buried beneath the bedclothes, no love to hold me near
There's no more songs and lullabies 'cos Sylvia's disappeared.

Buried beneath the bedclothes, I cry myself to sleep
Dare I come out of my hiding place, or shall I go back to sleep?
Dare I come out of hiding to peep beyond the sheets?
I wish I didn't have to see the things that frighten me
But I'll be brave and look again in the hope it's all a dream.
But what I see is real
It isn't a dream.

Surrounding walls of cold grey stone
Enormous and horrific shapes unfold

High above my bed a cable hangs suspended
A single light bulb with green metal shade
Soiled and tainted.

My head sideways turned on the pillow
A vertical window
The only source of natural light
With figure-painted panels that shine bright
Amidst the grey and gloom
Of this cellar room

I sit cross-legged upon my bed,
My back against the wall,
Six huge stone steps ahead of me
And a wooden door.
What's behind it, I don't know,
Where will it lead me? Out of here?

Determined to further search and explore
My eyes obey another call and like a bird
I stop, stare, and hold my breath.
Motionless, I focus, then ZOOM IN...
O dear God...my sister isn't here
Sylvia's not with me in this grey and gloom
No longer together...in this the cellar.

I have no memories of the year that followed my recovery, or
of what took place during the daily routine. I never thought of
Mama and Sylvia, which sounds awful, and makes me feel
guilty as I write. The only consolation is that it was not
deliberate, that looking back on it the temporary blackout in
my consciousness was nature's way of keeping me from going
insane. What remains indelibly on my mind is the endless
hours I spent looking at the huge grey slabs of stones piled
one on top of the other, held together by thickly pointed
cement. What was so fascinating as to hold my undivided
attention? At first it was not obvious, not until I became aware
of the subtle changes taking place in the colour of the stones.
The shade of grey of approximately a dozen or so chunks of
stone was lighter than the rest of the wall.

Soon, vague images began to appear and disappear on that part of the wall. There was no sense of fear, as in the past when this same wall had overpowered me with terror. On the contrary, as with each new day the images became more focused and pronounced, the greater the excitement became.

One day, totally unexpected, the most radiant faces appeared. So exquisite was their beauty that I cannot find words to do them justice. And, as the experiences continued day after day the wall and I developed a special bond. The stones had a life of their own and they held deep hidden secrets, some of which were being revealed and shared. I was able to communicate telepathically with my new-found friends, although I had no idea how this happened. It came to me as naturally as breathing.

My new friends would come and go of their own will, filling the room with love, a love that warmed me and drove the cold out of my small body. They created sweet-scented smells that filled the cellar and, when I laid my head down to sleep at night, the pillow had the fragrance of honeysuckle, which I identified years later. The adventure was beyond my wildest dreams, though at times I wondered whether I was not going mad.

During that year in solitary confinement, I often woke up drenched in perspiration, delirious, unable to know dream from reality. On one occasion, a nun stood at the side of the bed holding a wet cloth to my head. As I opened and closed my eyes I could see an enormous beam of light shining over us. The nun, transparent against the light, looked like an angel. I mentioned this to her days later, but she didn't know what I was talking about. She hadn't seen the beam of light.

I had many dreams. I visited other planets. Some were more pleasant than others. These dreams were in spectacular colours, hundreds of times brighter than any colours here on earth.

In one of the dreams, I was in prison and desperately wanted to get free, but hard as I tried I couldn't get away. A spirit suddenly appeared and said, 'Stop pushing at the door, it opens inwards. Close your eyes and imagine where you would most like to be if you were given the chance to leave the prison, and if you believe that you have the power, you will find yourself in the place of your choice.' I followed the advice and, although I can't remember how I got there, was pleasurably surprised to find myself outside the prison wall. I thanked the spirit, which said: 'I have shown you one of many tools to achieve freedom. Freedom is your birthright. Remember it always.'

That year I had many dream experiences. In one dream I was aware of the presence of a spirit whose softly-spoken voice I instinctively trusted and, although it wasn't possible to see him physically, as he had no form, I nevertheless knew that he was with me as we floated side-by-side high above the roofs and chimneys. But as my soul-body ventured even higher my feelings changed from a state of blissful calm to a bewildering uncertainty.

Below me, lying on the bed, quite still, was my body, which looked like a pale corpse. I wanted to get back in and reclaim it, but as I moved closer I had some doubts as to whether or not it would be possible to do so. The spirit friend told me, not by the spoken word but from his mind to mine, that I had nothing to fear, because he would protect my body from whatever evil spirits might try to invade it. Reassured by this, I went back in the direction from which I had come. I accelerated, though felt no movement as I flew on higher and higher into beautiful unknown regions of space.

I woke to find myself back in the cellar and in my body, which did not seem much of a surprise. Months later, by which time I had learned to move more easily into and out of my body, I was disappointed whenever my soul re-entered it. I felt let down. Going to sleep and dreaming had become an exciting nightly adventure.

Whatever the reason, God had decided to show such things in my dreams, and I shall be forever thankful for His treasured gift. Dreams had become part of my reality.

My Father Arrives

One day in February 1946 Sister Marie-Jeanne came into the cellar saying that the Mother Superior wanted to talk to me.

'How nice to see you again; please be seated,' the Mother Superior said. Memories of the last occasion when I had been in her office flooded my mind. Why was I here again?

I felt nervous and ill-at-ease, and without thinking, wiped the perspiration from my palms against the fabric covered armchair. Her expression conveyed disapproval, and I prayed that whatever the reason for my being there the visit would be over as quickly as possible.

'You've been with us for some considerable time. Let me see, it's been the best part of four years. My goodness! How time has flown, why, you were no more than an infant when we took you in. Look at you now, quite a grown-up girl.' She opened a folder on the desk, and ran her hands across the notes. 'You were too young then for me to have explained the reason why you were brought here, but now that you are older and circumstances have changed, I will explain it to you.'

I was furious, so angry I felt ready to explode. How dare she assume that Sylvia and I, having lived there more than half our lives, had never talked about it? Did she think I was a fool? And now, too late, she wanted to explain! I was so mortified that I decided not to listen to anything more, though had to come back from my own little world and acknowledge her presence.

'I hope what I have said will put your mind at rest; are there any questions you would like to ask?'

'No, nothing.'

'Are you quite sure?'

'Yes.'

'In that case I will ask him to come in.'

'Ask who to come in?'

She sighed deeply. 'Child, have you not heard a word of what I said?'

'I did...but...I didn't hear everything.'

'Your father is here.'

'My...father?'

I was shocked. I had no memory of him, and barely remembered what Sylvia had said about him. What would I say? Should I pretend to be happy? Would I like him? Would he like me? Why was he here and not Mama? I only wished Sylvia could be with me!

Mother Superior explained that my father had left Toulouse, and had served in the Belgian Merchant Navy from late 1940 until about mid 1942, during which time he had been instructed to carry a briefcase containing important documents. The ship had been torpedoed by the enemy and sunk. My father, with many other crew members, was stranded in the water in a life-jacket for hours before being picked up by the Royal Navy. As a result of this he was awarded a medal, and allowed to stay in England.

In September 1945 he came back to Belgium and began to look for Sylvia and me. Locating us proved so difficult that he hired a private detective, and returned to England to await results. Approximately five months later, he received news that I had been traced, and so came back to Belgium, in February 1946, with identification documents to prove that he was my father.

A tall slim figure with a dark beard and moustache came into the office with Sister Marie-Jeanne. He smiled, and with his arms outstretched, rushed towards me, picked me up and hurled me into the air, his beard brushing against my face and neck which felt sore and tender. I wanted him to let me go. He was so strong. Finally I laid my head on his shoulder. His beating heart against my body reminded me of the long sleepless nights when Sylvia and I had cuddled together in bed. It had been a long time since I had had any physical contact.

My hand moved across my father's face inquisitively. I played with his wavy black hair. Would he be very special? Would he love me the way Sylvia and I loved each other? Did he know Sylvia? If so, had he seen her or did he know where she was? Why hadn't he come sooner? So many questions filled my mind as he held me in his arms.

Leon moved to the window and gazed up at the sky. His brown eyes that had sparkled only moments ago were now filled with sadness. His hand was cold.

'Papa, why are you crying? You look like Jesus. He cried too when he was nailed to the cross.' He remained silent. Had I upset him? He exchanged glances with Mother Superior. 'Do you know my name?'

He replied, in a soft trembling voice. 'Of course, *chérie.*'

'What is it then?'

He smiled. 'Your name is Hava Leah Luftman Iglinski.' What little French he managed to speak was difficult to understand.

'Don't be silly! I don't have all those names.'

'Who said that to you?'

'No one. I'm just called Leah.'

'Please tell me, what education has my daughter had?'

'None, Monsieur. Your child was left here in our care. Our life here is dedicated to the teachings of our Lord Jesus Christ. Naturally this is what we have taught her. Monsieur, if you or the child's mother had not survived the war, she would have remained here and automatically would have taken up the vows of a novice. I believe we have served our purpose by having kept her hidden and safe from the Nazis.'

'Yes of course, you have been very kind. I am grateful. You have done everything humanly possible. Thank you very much. Did you remind Leah she is Jewish?'

'No Monsieur!'

'Well. Thank you again. I think I've taken up enough of your time. We have a long journey to make. I'll take Leah and go.'

Sister Marie-Jeanne handed him a small suitcase held together with a piece of rope. He helped me to put on a coat that I had never seen before. Although tight, and shorter than my dress, the novelty of wearing it simply delighted me. Sister Marie-Jeanne smiled and winked. Suddenly I hugged her and buried my head against her stomach. I clung to her robe, stricken with fear. Fear of leaving and fear of staying. What if she asked me to stay?

'I'll never forget you,' I whispered.

Papa bent down and buttoned my coat, removed his scarf and tied it loosely around my neck. I thought about Sylvia: We had arrived together, but I was leaving alone.

Both Mother Superior and Sister Marie-Jeanne were standing by the open wrought iron gates, waiting for us to go through.

It took a while to adjust to the outside world. I was mesmerised by the scenery, which was breathtakingly beautiful. I let go of Papa's hand and ran into the green open space of field and orchard. I twirled round and round in circles. The cool spring air felt wonderful and fresh. My face tingled. My short black curly hair blew in all directions. I looked back and saw Papa still talking with Mother Superior.

In the field nearby a herd of cows idly chewed the grass while others lay on their bellies. Tall trees with new buds reached towards the pale blue sky. A flock of birds glided high above my head in a V pattern, my eyes following them until the last one was out of sight.

The path through the field led into a small woodland area, and beyond on to a main road. The smell of pine mixed with sweet-scented flowers was everywhere. Later I was to learn the names of the flowers: yellow daffodils, purple, yellow and white crocuses, primroses and white snowdrops carpeted the shady woodland. Their lantern shapes seemed to give light along the path.

The base and roots of the trees were covered with green velvet moss. Frogs and toads leapt through the muddy foliage. I caught a baby frog and held it in my hands before it jumped away. Was everything going to be as beautiful as this?

We came to a main road. The bus arrived and we got on. The driver's face had deep lines and wrinkles. The skin on his face and hands was coarse and tanned. His black beret was tilted to one side of his forehead, partially hiding his receding hair. He handed Papa a ticket.

The choice of seats was ours, all but for the back row where an elderly couple slept. A teenage boy and an older woman sat near the entrance. They tore at a long stick of french bread, stuffed a thick bar of chocolate in the middle and ate the lot in one go. I licked my lips with envy.

We reached the outskirts of Brussels late in the afternoon. It was already dark outside. The tram terminal was busy. Crowds waited everywhere. We joined one. The rain was a halo of dazzling bright rays around the street gas-lights. The cobbled roads were crowded with noisy vehicles. Trams, trucks, bikes, cars hooted. Headlights glared through the fog and diesel fumes. My head throbbed and my throat was sore.

Trickling rain pitter-patter, ripples forming into puddles, and flowing over cobbled roads gurgling into drain. Crushed among a herd of people, I see worn soiled boots, shoes and slippers, people pushing shoving, oohing and aahing, tram wheels screeching to a halt and through windscreen wipers, faces peering, dull eyes numb with pain.

Papa holds my shoulders tight and thrusts me into the tram, bodies pressing all around me with suffocating odours. The tram ride long, my breath held, I can no longer keep from vomiting. Shouting...anger...spreading, and with the distance of each stop the amber faces step off.

5   Antwerp

The crowds, the noise the lights – it was all a nightmare from which Leah could not escape. People shuffled along taking one small step in front of the other, blindly following the person in front. They went on, dazedly, clutching their parcels.

Leah and her father managed to get a seat in the tram. Others, less fortunate stood in the overcrowded carriage. The man sitting opposite wore a large round black hat trimmed with fur. His bushy ginger beard spread over the upper part of his shirt and coat. His *peyot*[1] swayed as his body rocked back and forth. In his hand was an open book. The woman by his side slept, her hair covered by a brown scarf knotted and tied under her chin. The tram jerked to a halt, her head rolling slightly from the man's left shoulder. When she murmured something in her sleep, he leaned sideways and kissed her forehead. Seeing Leah looking at him, he smiled at the father and daughter.

'*Shalom aleichem*,' Leon said.

'What are you speaking?' Leah asked him.

'I can't explain it now,' he replied in his broken French.

'Then please speak in French.'

'It's easier for me to speak Yiddish.'

'Yiddish!... what's that?' she wanted to know, the ginger-haired man looking surprised at the question.

'How come the little girl doesn't understand Yiddish?' the man asked. His French was fluent with just a slight trace of an accent. 'Is she your daughter? I don't mean to pry, God forbid, my friend. It's just... what can I say... unheard of for a Jewish child especially in these parts not to speak Yiddish!'

'It's true, I know, but this bastard Hitler with his murdering

---

1 Sidelocks worn by Orthodox Jews.

33

barbaric pigs of…SS…what they did…my daughters had
to…'

He continued the conversation in Yiddish while the ginger-
haired man stroked his beard and now and then shook his
head in disbelief. 'Thank God you've found the little one.' His
eyes were kind and friendly as he went on talking in French,
perhaps so that Leah could follow.

'May the Almighty, blessed be His name, have saved my
wife…and my only child…a boy, Moishe…He will be
fifteen soon if the Almighty, blessed be His name has…' His
voice trembled: 'Liberation…was almost a year ago. I haven't
seen them in three years or more.'

He clasped his hands together and closed his eyes. His lips
opened and closed as he whispered to himself. Leah felt his
pain and wanted to put her arms around him, to tell him that
his family were alive, but she couldn't know that, so she
didn't say or do anything. She curled up to Leon and rested
her head on his arm.

'Papa, why has he and the other men here got ringlets and
big hats, and you haven't?'

'Why? Because they are religious Jews.'

'And you…are not?'

'No.'

'Why aren't you?'

'Why, why? Because I am not! I will explain some other
time, not now.'

'Rachel, wake up. We are almost here.'

The woman by the ginger-haired man's side rubbed her
eyes and straightened the scarf on her head.

'This is my sister Rachel.'

'I am pleased to meet you.' Leon smiled and they
exchanged a few words in Yiddish. Rachel's cheeks turned a
little pink and her eyelids lowered to the ground.

The ginger-haired man got up from his seat and reached up to
the wooden luggage rack. His voice was authoritative. 'Come
Rachel, help me to sort out these bags. Check that we have
everything. Nice talking to you both. I wish you the very best.'

'The same to you. *Shalom.*'

'*Shalom.*'

*

34

They had arrived in Antwerp. The rain had washed the cobbled streets and pavements clean. Gas lanterns shimmered against the deep blue night sky. The evening air was cold and damp.

'Leah, stop jumping in the puddles!'

'Why? But Papa, I've never jumped in a puddle before, I've never had fun like this! Why can't I?'

'Because I say so!'

'Why? What's wrong?'

'Your shoes and socks are wet and dirty!'

'So? I don't mind.' He stopped walking, lit a cigarette and pointing a finger at Leah, said, 'I mind arriving at my sister's home with you looking like this, dirty!'

'It's only my shoes and socks. I'm not dirty.'

'All right! Enough! Enough! Don't answer me back. I'm your father, you hear me!'

'But I'm only having a bit of fun. What's wrong with that?'

With lips firmly pressed together he glared at Leah, and walked off. Who was this stranger she had to live her new life with? Her stomach felt tight and knotted as she trotted behind him.

The surrounding buildings were in ruins, Leon looked sad and didn't speak. The walk led them through a tunnel. The only sound was the echo of their footsteps which reminded Leah of the church bells ringing and echoing through the cellar walls, which made her lose track of where she was. Before she had time to collect her thoughts, she was on the other side of the tunnel, in another noisy main street.

Women and men, young and old, strolled leisurely, arm-in-arm, while others held hands as they browsed at the shop windows. The brightly lit cafés and restaurants were filled with noisy people, loud music and smoke. Waiters manœuvred themselves around tables, balancing trays with one hand high above their shoulders. Musicians played accordions, harmonicas and guitars on the pavements.

Delicious smells of cooking came from all directions. Mobile kiosks stood at every street corner serving waffles and pancakes with a variety of savoury and sweet fillings. The women wore pretty dresses, shiny jewellery and high-heeled platform shoes with ankle straps, their red painted lips

35

smiling at the men walking by. Some of them kissed and hugged in open doorways.

'Hello love, you with the little girl, come back when you and your Missus have put her to bed. I've got something I think you'll enjoy,' the girl in the doorway said, winking and waving a bunch of keys in the air. Leon held Leah's hand and walked on briskly through the narrow streets.

'Do you know her? That pretty lady?'

'No.'

'Why did she say come back later? Will you?'

'Of course not. You mustn't talk to girls like that, they are bad!'

Leah looked over her shoulder at the woman. 'Bad? How? What do you mean?'

He held her hand and walked on. The female in the doorway was extraordinarily beautiful, a living fantasy that a man like Leon would dream of having at least once in a lifetime. She was young and vivacious. Under her open coat a low-cut dress revealed a cleavage of ample and voluptuous breasts. He imagined himself lost between her soft, warm flesh, gasping for breath while she smothered his face with her bosom, until her cries of ecstasy broke free like music to his ears.

Leah pulled at the sleeve of his coat: 'Why is that lady bad?'

'When you are older you will find out.' She was surprised at the distance they had walked.

'Ah, here we are in Lange Kievetstraat.'

They stopped in front of a small bay-windowed shop filled with pastel-coloured underwear. Leah, her face pressed against the glass, wished she could wear such pretty things.

Leon kissed his fingers and placed them on a gold object attached to the frame of the door.

'Why did you do that?' Leah asked, pointing towards it.

'I kiss it as a mark of respect to God. Inside of this, which is a Mezuza, is a prayer that blesses and protects whoever enters and leaves the home. It is an old Jewish custom.'

'Is it like the cross of Jesus that I kiss on my rosary?'

'What rosary?'

'Look, I'll show you.' When she put a hand inside her coat collar Leon exclaimed: 'No! Don't take it out here! We will throw it away when we are in the house.'

'I...I...don't want to throw it away.'

She was about to shed tears, when a light came on inside the shop. A woman's face peeped from behind the net curtains separating the window display from the shop floor.

'*Gott seidank*[1] you are both here, I was getting anxious. It's late, come in,' said Sara.

Leon's sister's hugs and kisses were brief, for she didn't like showing her emotions. Nevertheless, her heart was in the right place. She was the strong one of the family, honourable and reliable, a practical and level-headed woman who ran, single-handedly the household of one teenager and a frail, sick husband, as well as the hosiery shop.

Her husband Abraham sat in the same armchair and in the same position as in the morning when Leon had left the house to fetch Leah from the convent. His face was all sadness, his body emaciated. He was crying inside and Leon could feel his despair. He wanted to console him, but nothing he could say would change his fear and torment. His thoughts were far away, in Auschwitz and Buchenwald, secrets he could not share with any one.

Their eldest son Luzer, was sixteen. He had been murdered by the Nazis. Hanna, Abraham's only sister died in a camp.

Sara Eckstein, Leon's aunt, was his mother's sister. She married Nathan, a religious judge of the Jewish community in Antwerp. They had two daughters: Frieda the eldest, aged fourteen and Fanny aged nine.

Mosche, Leon's brother, married Mania, and Charles their son was born in Paris in 1936.

The immediate family counted twenty living members before the Nazi round-up of Jews started in 1942. Eight were caught and deported, Abraham was the only one who survived the ordeal.[2]

Charles, Sara's and Abraham's son, was a handsome, intelligent and confident fourteen-year-old, who had been hidden in various places in Belgium. He and his sister Dena, a young woman of twenty-one, were the pride and joy of their parents, the focus of everything that summed up their lives.

---

1 Thank God.
2 Luzer, Hanna, Sara, Nathan, Frieda, Fanny and Moshe were all arrested and deported by the Nazis, and died in various camps.

During the Nazi occupation, Dena and her mother Sara had been hidden in Brussels by a doctor and his family, and in 1945, after the liberation, Dena had left the family home for Palestine.

Sara had been worried, not knowing what to expect of Leah's condition when she arrived, but to her joy and relief found her niece in reasonably good health. Charles had been delighted on hearing that Leah was coming to stay for a couple of weeks. It brought back pleasant memories for everyone, of the time before the war when the children spent much of the afternoon playing together. In those days Charles had been appointed 'chief babysitter' by Frania, Leah's mother, not because he was the second eldest in the family circle, which had little to do with it, but because Frania admired his caring nature combined with a happy disposition. Besides, Sylvia and Leah adored him.

Charles fussed over Leah as if she was his younger new-found sibling, and even went so far as to cut the food on her plate into small portions, showing her how to use a knife and fork correctly. He also taught her how to keep the area between the plate and the table free from bits of food.

At first, everyone found it difficult to understand how remarkably well-adjusted and at ease Leah was right from the start with the family. Her appetite, thank God, was normal, and she ate everything put before her. On the Sabbath, Abraham poured a drop of red wine into each glass, while Leon cut the *challah*.[1] When Sara made the blessings over the candles in Leah's presence for the first time, Leah took the rosary from under the collar of her dress and kissed it.

'When Sister Marie-Jeanne lit the candles in the chapel I always had to kiss the rosary,' she explained, smiling.

'Take this thing off!' Leon said, reaching over for the rosary.

'No! It's mine.' Leah shrank back into the chair and put the rosary back around her neck. Sara's heart seemed to break when she saw the pain in Leon's eyes, and spoke in Yiddish so that Leah wouldn't understand.

'*Oy*, my poor brother, I want to help resolve this without causing any further problems. You've got enough to cope with

---

1 A special plaited bread for the Sabbath dinner.

and you need this, on top of everything else, like a hole in the head.'

She filled the ladle with soup and poured it over the bowl of noodles, *kneidlech*,[1] carrots, butter beans, and parsnips. Charles got up to help take the chicken soup around the table, serving his father, as was customary for the head of the family, before anyone else. Then came the guests – a tradition of respect and good manners that Sara both liked and kept.

'She is used to the rosary, I don't think you should force it away from her,' Charles said.

'What are you talking about!' Leon responded, between spoonfuls of chicken soup. 'She is Jewish! The sooner we all make it clear to her the better.'

'It might confuse her,' Charles told him.

'O God! A fourteen-year-old is telling me what is right and wrong!'

'No, Uncle Leon, I am only giving my opinion.'

'If I wanted your opinion I would ask for it.'

Abraham cleared his throat, and placed his spoon on the side of the soup bowl. Everyone kept quiet. He passed the napkin around his mouth, dabbing it gently several times, and with his eyes fixed briefly on each of them in turn, said, 'I suggest that you leave her alone with this business of the rosary. After all, what difference does it make at this stage? She's well, and she's a lovely girl. That's what counts, surely?'

Tension round the table made Charlie lose his appetite, so he kept Leah amused, cutting up left-over vegetables from the soup bowl into small pieces to decorate a *kneidlech*. He then took a layer of salt and diced butter beans to make eye-sockets, and used a tiny ball of squashed leak to form the nose. A sliced carrot became a mouth and, to top it all, a pile of egg noodles covered the crown of the *kneidlech* with strands and twists for knots, which hung like an ornamental headdress.

'Are you *meschuga*?'[2] Leon said, 'And in the meantime I should be humiliated and embarrassed by everyone I come in contact with?' He lifted the napkin from his lap, wiped his mouth, and slapped it back on to the table. He paced up and

---

1 Round dumpling.

2 Crazy

down, puffing and blowing on his cigarette. The room went silent, the children apprehensive.

'I'll try and talk with her tomorrow,' Sara said, 'tonight is already too late. Come and sit down and eat, we should be rejoicing at Leah's homecoming. It's Shabbat, so let's make it pleasant and talk of *simchas*[1] and the future of our children, of the Promised Land to where maybe one day we will emigrate and be with Dena and our people.'

Leon sat down, and Sara served the main course of roast chicken, *latkes*[2] and red cabbage, placing it in the middle of the table. Abraham spoke calmly, 'Give her time to observe and learn the Jewish customs, and slowly, slowly you will see when she is secure. The rosary believe me, will be forgotten. She's a baby still. All this is new to her.'

'A baby? She's a young girl!' Leon insisted.

'That's not what Abraham means,' Sara said. 'Basically he is saying "try to be more patient". There are other priorities besides the rosary, that require serious consideration, like teaching her to write, taking her out gradually so she can mingle and talk to local people and shopkeepers. She needs to be stimulated and encouraged to do things, maybe to play with Dena's old toys that I've kept. All sorts of things that will help to build her confidence. At the moment everything must seem strange and new to her, and very confusing I would think.'

'All right! You're the woman and you know more about these things than I do. And Abraham, you've been a father longer than me, so I will take your suggestions too.'

Leon was determined to leave after a few days, to try to find Sylvia, even though he had little information concerning her whereabouts. Mother Superior had not known where she was. The last thing she had heard was that Sylvia had been transferred several times after being taken away from the convent.

'When will you be back, Papa?'

'In a few days.'

'When is a few days? Show me on my fingers.' Leon wasn't sure how to respond to Leah's proposal, so Sara intervened, suggesting that with Leah's fingers and hers

---

1 Celebration.
2 A special kind of grated and fried potato cakes.

together, that would be about the number of days before Leon would come back.

'And you promise to bring Sylvia? Promise! Promise, Papa.' Poor Leon couldn't speak, though knew that his silence agitated Leah. He couldn't help it, and looked at Sara furtively, apparently wanting her to help him out of this delicate situation, so she said to her: *'Chérie,* your Papa will do his very best to find Sylvia. And if he finds her he will bring her here.'

'What does that mean, you will do your very best? Why can't you promise that he will bring Sylvia here?' Leah persisted.

'We shall have to wait and see when your Papa comes back,' Sara said. 'We wish you a safe and speedy return, Leon, and pray to God you will have *mazel*[1] and find Sylvia.'

They stood on the cobbled pavement in front of the shop and waved until Leon was out of sight.

During the week, Charles was at school from eight o'clock in the morning till one o'clock, and Leah was happy to stay with Sara in the shop. One day, she held a satin slip against her cheeks and asked, 'Where is Mama?'

'I wish I knew *Chepsela,*[2] come to me and sit on my lap. I hope to hear from people who knew your mama during the war, when she and I and the family lost contact with one another. These people might know where she is.'

'Oh! You really think so? I miss my Mama and I want to be with her. I love you as well, Tante Sara but…but you're Charlie's Mama, not mine.'

'I love you too, very very much.'

Sara held Leah close in her arms and rocked her back and forth. She imagined the situation reversed with her own son Charles, God forbid, and her Dena, in Leah's position. It could so easily have happened. Thank God they had been spared this agony.

After school, Leah would be with Charles while he did his homework, and at this time she began to draw with coloured crayons. Everyone was delighted to discover that her

---

1. Luck.
2. Little dear.

41

drawings showed not only a good eye for colour but also a fertile imagination.

After Sara locked up the shop in the evening, Leah would join the family. She often placed herself by the side of Abraham's armchair, in which he had sat day in, day out, from dawn until dusk, since his liberation from Auschwitz a year ago. Impossible to say what drew her to Abraham's side. Sara would never know. She gently touched his face with delicate fingers, her other hand held in his, a mutual love and understanding that barely required more than a few simple words between them.

Most evenings, Charles' parents went to bed early, and he read bedtime stories to Leah. She particularly enjoyed looking through the nature book of animals, her favourites being the apes and monkeys. Her radiant face would encourage Charles to go on reading late into the night.

'Charlie, look at the monkey's big red bottom. Doesn't it look horrid?' Leah burst out laughing, then paused for a moment as she inspected both sides of her own hands and feet, comparing them with those of the primates in the book. 'Let me see your hands and feet Charlie.'

Her eyes moved inquisitively from one hand and foot to the other, from hers to his, then back to those in the book, till she cheerfully exclaimed, 'They have the same hands and feet as you and me, Charlie. How come?'

Her eyes were underlined by dark shadows, due to fatigue from having stayed up so late. Nevertheless, they sparkled with excitement and intrigue at her discovery. After the first sentence of Charles' explanation (a rather poor version of the history of evolution) Leah had fallen asleep, her rag doll 'Jacquie' clasped to her cheek.

My dear sister Sylvia was home. But there were no happy smiles, no hugs, no words. There was complete silence as she stood staring across Tante Sara's living room. Her face, pale and thin, was not the one I remembered. I ran to her, held her hand and kissed it. Sylvia didn't move. She slowly freed her hand from mine, and let it drop heavily against her side. Her large brown eyes were glazed, as if she were looking through clouds of smoke.

'Sylvia! It's me, Leah.'

'It's good to see you.'

'It's lovely to see you too, Sylvia. I've missed you so much. Where have you been?'

She paused. 'I don't want to talk about it. I just want to forget...all of it.'

'You will, Sylvia. You will. You're not there anymore, so it's OK. I'm so happy that we're together again!'

'I'm very tired. I'd like to lie down.'

'Can I come and lie down with you like we used to?'

'I'd rather be on my own right now.'

'But why, Sylvia? We always used to go to bed together and cuddle.'

'Please excuse me, everyone, I hope you won't think me rude but I need to sleep. I have a headache.' Her voice was as gentle and calm as I had remembered it. She got up from the chair and left the room. Papa followed her.

6   Gucia's Story

The days passed quickly for Leon in his sister Sara's home. He was getting ready to leave for England. He had applied to the Belgian authorities for passports for Sylvia and Leah, but the bureaucratic system required convincing evidence of his wife's consent.

At that time, he had not yet found out where Frania was, or even whether she was still alive. Not being able to find her whereabouts complicated matters.

Their relationship had been difficult, and after the separation in early 1940, he left the family home in Rue Jolly, to stay in another part of Brussels with his brother Jack, and his sister-in-law Paula, before going to Toulouse. But he had kept in contact, and occasionally visited her and the children in Bleekery Strasser, Antwerp.

When he left for England, at the end of 1940, they exchanged letters for a time, but the Nazi occupation of Belgium made it impossible for their correspondence to continue, until all contact between family members was lost.

Sara had prepared a dinner party for a family reunion, and among them was Clara, Leon's youngest sister, her husband Simon, and their five-year-old daughter Evelyn. There was Jack, Leon's brother, his wife Paula and their three-year-old daughter Denise. And Gucia. Gucia was one of Leon's sisters-in-law, Frania's older sister, and Leon had not seen her for six years. She had survived Auschwitz, and told them that evening how Frania and herself had been in the same barracks, and that like so many young and pretty inmates, Frania had been used by the SS and died shortly after her arrival. Once the emigration department accepted Gucia's explanation of Frania's death, they gave Leon his daughters' passports.

Sylvia, unlike her cousins and her sister, was a quiet and

self-contained child who spoke only when spoken to and kept her replies brief and to the point. She spent most of her days avidly reading books and newspapers. Leon was happy and proud of her intelligence, and of her ability to study on her own. One day, shortly after their reunion Leah said, 'Sylvia, please play with me today.'

'I will soon, Leah, I just want to read a bit longer.'

'You say that every day, but you never play with me.' Upset and furious, I was convinced she no longer loved me. 'You're such a spoilsport and a misery. Just you wait and see when you want me to play with you. I hate you! I wish Papa had never found you. I wish he would take you back to wherever you came from. You're trying to stop me from having fun. Just because you're unhappy, you want me to be unhappy too. Well, I won't be! You're jealous because Charlie is my friend and not yours. Well it's your own fault... Anyway, I'm never going to talk to you again. So there!'

Sylvia left the room, crying. And Papa followed her. Next day Leon took both girls out shopping in Antwerp.

Leon and his daughters met Tante Gucia and her children in a restaurant near the central station, on Simon Straat, where Gucia (Shaina Golda) had found temporary accommodation. Her eldest daughter Sarah was twelve, Fanny was eleven (the same age as Sylvia) and Yosi, her son, was five.

It was reasonably early when they arrived at the restaurant, and the lunchtime trade had not yet begun. A few customers browsed through newspapers over cups of coffee, some having a small glass of spirit with their hot drink. The waiter brought each of the children a large oblong glass piled high with strawberry, chocolate and vanilla ice cream, topped with chocolate sauce dripping over the brim and on to the wafer biscuits and plate. It was a special treat for them, and while Sylvia scooped the tiniest amount of ice cream on to her spoon, Leah and her cousins giggled and dipped into each others' bowls. Leon and Gucia sipped their lemon tea, ate cheese-cake, smoked cigarettes, and talked continuously in a mixture of French and Yiddish whenever they didn't want the children to understand.

Sylvia listened with great interest as Gucia told Leon what

had happened to her and her family before and during the war.

'In 1929 my parents, Itta and Schlomo, came to live in Belgium. My brothers and sisters came too. Joel, Frania, Paula, myself and our brother Jacob. We were sad to leave our home in Wloclawek, and our friends. But Frania must have told you this when you were married to her.'

'Yes, some of it. But you can tell me again.'

'Well, like all the other Jews, we left to get away from anti-Semitism and from the thieves that stole the furs from my parents' workshop – and whatever else they could get their hands on. My parents believed that for the Jews, life in Western Europe was better than in Poland. I was eighteen at the time. A couple of years later, as you know, I married Jacob Mendlewicz.'

'Yes.'

'He worked hard as a haberdashery salesman, travelling around the country. In 1935 when Fanny, my second child was born, I became very sick and lost a lot of weight. The doctor didn't know what was wrong with me. When Fanny was six weeks old, we took her to a foster family who lived in a village called Wilrijk, a suburb here in Antwerp.'

'Then in 1942 Jacob was ordered by the Germans to work in France. We believed, as did so many others, that it was a genuine work assignment, but of course, it was slave-labour in a concentration camp. Before leaving for France, Jacob had asked whether I'd manage on my own to look after our two children. I felt sure that I could. Later, I was unable to cope and took my eldest daughter Sarah and my year-old son Yosi to join Fanny at the Christian foster family. Frania and I then stayed at alternative addresses: 2 Rue Jolly, Brussels, belonged to a friend of hers, a Monsieur Brinier, and 47 Rue Jolly – the apartment you both lived in before you separated. My parents had already been deported to Auschwitz on 29 August 1942. Before that, Frania and my parents had taken Sylvia and Leah to a hiding place, a convent. After the children were safely hidden, Frania and I managed to keep ourselves hidden from the Nazis. What happened then was the unimaginable.'

'Frania and I were having dinner one night – we were at 47 Rue Jolly – when suddenly there was violent knocking and the door flew open – it was the Gestapo. We were taken to a transit camp in Mechelen. It was 10 February 1943. We remained there for six weeks. On 19 April we were all forced into a very long cattle train. It seemed like thousands of us. We were locked in, squashed like sardines. We didn't know where they were taking us. There was no one to ask. We were going through the countryside at night when the train suddenly shrieked to a halt. We could hear the German guards running alongside the train, shouting at the top of their voices, apparently not knowing why the engineer had stopped the train. They were asking 'Who put this red light on the tracks?' Eventually, we understood from their shouts that one of the wagons had been forced open from the outside and some of our people were escaping. There was some shooting, then silence, then the journey went on. When the train stopped again, we were in Auschwitz.'

The following information is based on facts which I received from the Joods Museum van Deportatie en Verzet, Mechelen, Belgium, of the train journey Convoy XX to Auschwitz, on the night of 19 April 1943. A document shows the names of Frania (my mother) and Gucia listed on transport, Convoy XX.

For Love of Life

Boortmeerbeek, 19 April 1943: A unique act of heroism

There is no doubt about it that during the summer of 1941 the information offices of the Allied countries knew about the genocide on the Jews by the Nazis. Why didn't the Allied troops do anything to stop this judeocide by, for example, bombing the railways or important railway junctions? This is, even today, a controversial matter. Also the organised resistance groups didn't take any action, because of reasons of feasibility and practicality, to stop the transport of Jews anywhere in Europe. That is why the event in Boortmeerbeek on 19 April 1943 is so unique in the history of the deportations.

Mechelen, 19 April, 1943: the assembly of the twentieth convoy. Around 9 p.m. train N801 leaves the Dossin barracks, direction Auschwitz. The train consists of forty wagons, 'cattle truck'-type 'eight horses or 40 men'– containing 1631 deportees. Forty armed guards from the '*Schutzpolizei*' are situated in the first and last wagon.

At about 11 p.m. the train slows down as the railroad bends between Boortmeerbeek and Haacht, direction Leuven. It is there where three young men raid the train. The initiator is Youra Livschitz (17 September 1917), a young Jewish physician from Brussels. He gets help from two school friends, Jean Franklemon and Robert Maistriau.

To stop the train, they put a red hurricane-lamp on the rails. When the Belgian engine driver notices the red light, he stops the train immediately. Livschitz jumps in front of the locomotive, holding a light revolver, to stop it going any further. The unarmed Franklemon gets caught by a German guard, but he struggles free and runs away. At the same time Maistriau opens a wagon, using a flashlight and pincers. He shouts to the surprised Jewish deportees that they have to jump out of the train and hide themselves in the surrounding fields. Only seventeen passengers dare to jump; Maistriau quickly gives them some money and indicates the direction of Brussels. He wants to open a second wagon, but the German guards approach and they have to flee. The train goes on.

At the border with Germany it seems that a total of 231 prisoners escaped. They jumped out of the moving train. This was possible because the Belgian engine driver slowed down before reaching the border. Sometimes the jump was fatal: the day after, 23 bodies were found by the railroad tracks, together with eight badly wounded persons.

In May 1993, on the 50th anniversary of this event, a commemorative plaque was unveiled at the railway station (Boortmeerbeek). Every year, around 19 April, a memorial ceremony takes place.

Gucia's Story

Mechelen, July 24, 2000,

Dear Madam Goodman,

Here are the answers to your letter of 16 July 2000.

1) You received a copy of the original *Transportliste* of the XXth transport from Malines to Auschwitz. The date that you can see in the left corner is the date of arrival and inscription in the transit camp Malines. The persons could be arrested on the same day, or some days before and be held by the Gestapo.
2) The date of departure from Malines to Auschwitz was 19 April 1943.
3) The sisters Frania and Szajna Golda IGLINSKI stayed for six weeks in the SS-Sammellager Mechelen before being deported to Auschwitz.
4) The XXth train left Malines on 19/04/1943 and arrived in Auschwitz on 22104/1943.
5) I confirm also by these that we sent you two years ago an article titled: 'A Unique Act of Heroism'.

You can always mail or write me if you'd like more explanation.

Sincerely yours,

Miss Laurence Schram,
Searcher and Archivist,
Jewish Museum of Deportation en Resistance,
Goswin de Stassartstraat, 153,
2800 Mechelen – Belgium
E-mail: infos@cicb.be

'Please Gucia, don't tell me what went on inside the camp.'

'I won't, Leon. I was recently told that in March 1944 the foster father of the Christian family was arrested by the Nazis and sent to Buchenwald concentration camp for helping to save Jewish children. Sarah, Fanny and Yosi for safety reasons were placed in a children's orphanage home in Brussels. There, Sarah caught typhus and was transferred to a hospital run by nuns. Fanny was sent to a different children's home and Yosi remained in the children's home in Brussels.'

'In 1945 the foster father survived the ordeal in Buchenwald, and the children were reunited with their Christian family. Sometime after liberation I went to the village and stayed with my children and the foster family for about ten months. I had no money, nowhere to live, and I didn't know what had happened to my husband. Later, I took the children to the Zionist Federation children's home in the centre of Antwerp.'

'Many children there were on their way to Palestine. My brother Joel, who had left Belgium in 1936, is in Palestine and has written to me asking if I would let the children go to him where he promised to look after them on a Kibbutz in Negba. I have agreed to let them go to Palestine and stay with my brother Joel on Kibbutz Negba, thinking that I will follow as soon as I know what has happened to Jacob.'

'Do you know yet what has happened to your sister Paula and your brother Jacob?' Leon asked.

'On the evening of Paula's wedding, the Gestapo had her and her husband deported to Auschwitz. Paula was just twenty-one years old. She and her husband didn't survive and my brother Jacob also died in Auschwitz.'

Leon put his arm around Gucia's shoulder. 'O my God! You mean... All the family was murdered!'

'Yes. And I don't know how I survived. What my eyes have witnessed will haunt me all the days of my life. Thank God our children are alive. And that they're in reasonably good health, I am more than grateful.'

'Yes, you are right. Tell me, where are you living in the meantime?'

'I have a small two-room place above a photographer's shop near here. It's not much but it's better than nothing. It will do for now until I go to Palestine.'

1. Grandma Itta, Grandpa Szlojme, with their children Frania (left), Joel (centre) and Gucia (right). Photograph taken in Poland, 1912.

2. Father Leon and Sylvia in Brussels, Belgium, 1935.

3. Mother, with Sylvia, Belgium, 1935.

4. Mother's brother, Joel, in Europe before leaving for Palestine in 1936.

5. Mother's sister, Aunt Pesa (or Paula), who was murdered in Auschwitz. She was deported on the eve of her wedding. Photograph taken in Belgium, 1942.

6. Cousin Charles, Sarah (Leon's sister) and Uncle Abraham, who escaped both from Belsen and Auschwitz. Photograph taken in 1946.

7. Sylvia, aged 11 years, and Leah, aged seven years. Photograph taken in Antwerp, a few days before emigrating to London. Belgium, 1946

8. Mother's eldest sister, Gucia, escaped from Auschwitz. She is photographed here in 1946 with her children Sara (standing at the back, left) and Fanny (standing at the back, right). In front, from left to right, are Sylvia, Leah and Yosi.

9. Blankenberg, Belgium. Back row (left to right): Leah, Evelyn and Denise; front row, both cousins called Albert. 1948.

10. Father and Leah at Blankenberg, Belgium.

11. Blankenberg, Belgium. Left to right: Leah, Aunt Clara and Evelyn.

12. Leah in Tunbridge Wells, Kent, 'The Beacon, taken around 1947.

13. The family grave in East Ham Cemetary, London.

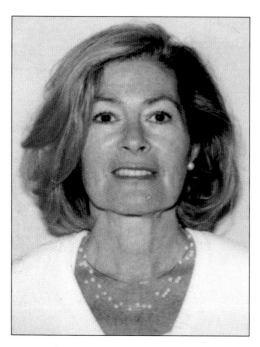

14. Leah Iglinski-Goodman, 2000.

'What happened to Mama?' Sylvia asked suddenly. Leon and Gucia looked at each other, horrified.

'We don't know yet, *chérie*,' Gucia replied, stroking her niece's cheek.

'She is alive, isn't she?' Sylvia asked.

'We hope so, *chérie*. We'll find out, but it might take some time before we know.' She didn't have the heart to tell her the truth. God only knew, she would find out soon enough!

'Come, let's go and do our shopping,' Leon said. Gucia was grateful for the suggestion. Leah and her three cousins ran out of the restaurant while Leon paid the cashier.

'Tante Gucia I'm almost as tall as you. Look, my shoulder nearly reaches yours.' Sylvia and Gucia were walking arm-in-arm behind Leon, 'Yes, *chérie*, you are going to be tall like your father. On my side of the family we are all small but with big hearts.'

Gucia squeezed Sylvia's arm. Her blue eyes were full of life and sparkled. Her dark brown hair, cut short, was thick and wavy. No one would ever guess by looking at her what Gucia had gone through, nor did her dress give a clue as to how poor she was. They left the restaurant and took a short tram ride to another shopping area.

The day was very special. Leon bought Sylvia and Leah each an entire wardrobe of clothes, underwear, dresses, blouses, skirts, jumpers, socks and shoes. He meticulously chose and inspected each item, insisted that they tried on everything and checked that the clothes fitted well. They left the shop with Sylvia and Leah wearing a new outfit. Sylvia was thrilled with her new blue woollen dress: it looked quite grown-up with its long sleeves, button cuffs, two pleats on both front and back of the skirt, deep blue embroidery at the front, and blue stitches around the edge of the collar and belt. And on top of everything, Leon had bought her a watch.

Gucia took them to the photographic shop below her rooms where they had a family photo taken. Leon didn't want to be in it. At the same time, they had photos taken of Sylvia and Leah together. Sylvia felt sad about leaving and saying goodbye to Gucia and her cousins, but Leon promised they would see one another again before Gucia left for Palestine. 'Maybe we can spend the summer holidays together in

Blankenberg with the rest of the family like we use to. Remember?' he said smiling.

7 Journey to England

In March 1946 Leon, Sylvia and Leah left Sara's home in Lange Kievstrasse for England. At Brussels airport passports and boarding cards were checked on the runway.

'Where is your other child?' asked the ground hostess. 'She...' Leon paused and turned around. There were twenty or more people in the queue but no sign of his daughter Leah. His heart beat fast. Each rhythmic beat vibrated louder than the last from his chest up to his temple. It frightened him. What if he died? Who would take care of his children? He had not considered death before, nor made provision for such an eventuality. His thoughts were interrupted by the hostess. 'Monsieur, will you please tell me if the child is with you?'

'Yes...she is.' His voice was faint, drawn out words trembling on his lips.

'*Chérie*... did... you... see... where ... your sister... went?'

'No Papa.'

'Monsieur, will you and your daughter please stand back so that other passengers can board the plane?' The hostess indicated with her hand where they should stand, at which precise moment Leon was convinced that his vision and his hearing were deceiving him. He could not believe his eyes and ears. Was it really his daughter at the entrance to the plane jumping, waving and shrieking?

'Sylvia! Papa! Hurry! Quick! This is like a big bird with lots of seats inside its tummy.' Sylvia giggled. Leon took off his trilby and wiped the perspiration from his forehead. The ground hostess smiled and handed the boarding cards back to him. 'I hope you have a pleasant flight,' she said, winking at Sylvia.

After the announcement that the safety belts could be removed, Leon let Sylvia and Leah kneel on their seats, then sat back and closed his eyes. But he could not sleep.

'*Bonjour*, monkey-man, *bonjour*,' Leah said, smiling

enthusiastically at a black man sitting in the seat behind her.

He gently patted the tips of her fingers clinging to the back of her seat. '*Bonjour*, little girl and what is your name?'

'The monkey-man is talking...did you hear him? did you?' she squeaked.

The slap on the back of her legs stung, and brought tears to her eyes. She curled down into her seat and hid with embarrassment.

'Don't hit me, or I will hit you back,' she said, trying not to cry.

'You are very rude. You cannot call someone a monkey. Where did you learn such a thing? From the convent?'

'No.'

'Sit there and be quiet,' Leon warned, standing up to face the man behind: 'I am very sorry the way my daughter spoke with you, please accept my apologies.'

'Oh, it is nothing. She meant no harm, and I've not taken offence. I have three children of my own and their innocent remarks often take me by surprise, too,' said the man, chuckling.

'You had better learn to stop answering Papa back like that, otherwise you will always be in trouble with him,' Sylvia whispered.

'But that's not fair. He didn't let me tell him how I know that is a monkey-man.'

'So tell me instead.'

'Charlie showed me the monkey in the book, that's how.'

'Oh I see, probably the book showed how we came from apes and monkeys to being humans. But that man is not a monkey, he is the same as Papa and that man over there, and there. The only difference is the colour of his skin,' Sylvia explained.

'But why does he look like the monkeys in the book?'

'When we get to England we will buy a book which will explain it all.'

'That will be good, won't it Sylvia?' Leah's attention was quickly diverted as she peeped over the seat, sheepishly smiling at the man who understood that this was her way of wanting to communicate with him. He smiled back.

'Can I sit with you?' she asked.

'Of course you may.' He helped her on to the seat next to him. Whatever it was that they shared together, it made them laugh a lot.

'Look at all that white fluff outside the window. We're flying in heaven,' she announced to everybody. One woman was overheard saying, 'Isn't the imagination of a child wonderful!'

People sitting nearby talked among themselves while others laughed at the various comments.

'Can you imagine if we were all on our way to heaven? That would certainly be something to write home about,' another passenger remarked. The white clouds had vanished, and they were flying through a pool of blue space, Leah wishing she could be in it forever. 'Will we get to heaven soon?'

The black man laughed softly, his body bouncing up and down like a ball. 'You need not concern your pretty little head with such things yet. One day we will all go to heaven. That is a guarantee my child.' He patted her hand and began to laugh again. 'Oh yes, and don't you go forgetting what I just said.'

Sylvia, had fallen asleep next to Leon, and was woken by a voice over the loudspeaker. 'Please fasten your seat belts. We are scheduled to land in fifteen minutes, but due to unexpected turbulence there may be some delay. On behalf of the pilot and myself we hope you have had a comfortable flight and we thank you for flying with Sabena Airlines.'

A flash of lightning was followed by thunder, some of the passengers screaming with fear as the aircraft swayed to one side and then the other. '*Chérie*, are you OK? Just sit still, we will be safe in just a little while.'

'I'm OK Papa. I'm not frightened. I just don't like thunder and lightning,' Leah explained from the row behind. Through the windows you could see the sky covered by dark grey clouds, while on the opposite side the sky was blue. The contrast was amazing, and Sylvia was fascinated. 'How does that happen Papa?'

The plane suddenly banked and her ears became blocked. The wheels touched the runway in London, and the engine roared, flaps on both wings going down as the plane glided on to the tarmac, finally coming to a halt by the terminal building.

'Are we in heaven now?' Leah asked. No one said anything, though there were many smiling faces.

8   Clarendon Place

Leon and the children arrived at Clarendon Place, in Bayswater, to a double room on the ground floor which he had rented long before leaving for Belgium. From the large window you looked on to both the side street and the main Bayswater road bordering Hyde Park.

The room was spacious, orderly and well-kept, furnished with a rich gold-coloured walnut wardrobe, a tallboy, a dressing table, a sofa-bed, a portable electric cooker, a fridge, table and chairs, curtains and rugs, all belonging to Leon. In the centre of the dressing table was an embossed silver hand-mirror, brush and comb set, and on either side were two prominent enlarged photographs in silver frames, one of a woman and child, the other of a small girl.

'Who is this Papa?'

'Why, *chérie*, this is Sylvia when she was about two or three years old.'

'I don't remember having curly hair, I look quite nice there,' Sylvia commented proudly.

'Nice! My *chérie* you were beautiful, just as you are now,' Leon replied affectionately.

'This is my Mama? O Papa isn't she pretty?' Leah said.

'Yes she was, I mean she is,' he corrected himself as he unpacked their clothes from the suitcase and placed them neatly on the wardrobe shelves. Leah held the frame close and quietly examined the photograph. Her lips gently touched the glass, then she held the photo in an embrace.

'Papa, is this me with Mama in this picture?' she asked happily.

'No, *chérie*, this is also Sylvia with Mama when Sylvia was, *oy vey*! such a healthy, fat baby.'

'Oh, where is a picture of Mama and me then?'

'I don't have one.'

'Why?'

'I don't know exactly.'

'Because you and Mama liked Sylvia better than me?'

'No, don't say that,' said Sylvia. 'They loved us both the same.' She explained that their mother must have kept her photos with Leah for herself. But nothing she said could take away Leah's terrible hurt. But while Leah struggled with her emotions she sensed a sudden nudge. Images came into her mind. It was, as it had often been during her stay in the cellar, no more than a subtle feeling or an idea that would float into her mind. Her response was intuitive and immediate. She knew without understanding how, that the inner 'guidance' was there. Standing in front of the dressing-table mirror, she held the photograph of her mother to her cheek. The reflection of her mother and herself together at that moment was the turning point that made her painful ordeal bearable.

Constant change became a way of life, and Leon found he had not anticipated the problems involved in the everyday running of a home for two young girls.

One night, long after Sylvia and Leah were in bed, he continued working into the early hours of the morning. He had to finish the suit before Mr Abramovitch, a private client, whose grandson was having his bar-mitzvah at the weekend, arrived for the final fitting.

Leon remembered the times when he and Frania were happy. She had been his first love, from the moment he had set eyes on her sitting in a kosher restaurant in Tomaszow with members of her family. The vegetable and barley soup dripped from the edge of his spoon, down the side of his mouth and chin as his hand shook while staring at her from behind a newspaper. Everything about her appealed to him: her large brown eyes, the fullness of her lips, and the dark wavy hair hanging below her shoulders. He liked the way she used her eyes and hands to express herself. When she and her family stood up and left the restaurant he thought he'd never see her again but, three years later, they met in a popular café-bar in Antwerp. Both families had moved to Belgium. Soon they were madly in love, and a year later they married.

Frania gave him two lovely children. Leon loved both the

girls, but was haunted by doubts as to whether Leah was really his. The question still tormented him. 'I will go to the grave not knowing the truth! Damn it!' he said out loud, guiding the thread through the hole of the needle and telling himself that if he had not been unfaithful on so many occasions they might not have had such awful fights and become separated. It had all been his fault. It was shaming to think about, and his stomach was so curdled he thought that at any moment he might throw up. Had he not strayed, he would have had no motive or reason to become so eaten with jealousy, because Frania would not have been seeing another man. He had begged for her forgiveness and they were reconciled, but then she was pregnant again!

He could think of many reasons why the relationship went wrong the second time, but their decision to separate, two years later, had cost him dearly. He tried to reconstruct the circumstances of her death in Auschwitz, but all his emotions became entangled with fatigue, fear and guilt.

'If I had not left, she would still be alive! And the children would not have suffered! Ah, hell! This bitchy life!' he muttered. His bones ached. He had sat too long in one position. His neck and shoulders were stiff. His eyes itched and he had to rub them. Standing up, he stretched and wiped the sweat from his face.

The whirring of the electric Singer sewing machine, the whistling spout of the kettle, the sudden change of tone on the radio, the glaring lights – all stopped Sylvia and Leah from sleeping well.

Sylvia got out of bed and stood by his chair. 'Papa, I can't sleep. I am so tired, but when I fall asleep I'm woken up again. Must you work late every night? Have you nearly finished now?'

He held her hand, kissed her on the nose and sighed deeply, not knowing what to say.

She stood on tip-toe and reached for his robe hanging on a brass hook at the back of the door. As she rolled up the sleeves her thin and delicate arms waved inside the grey and maroon silk dressing gown. She tied the belt firmly into a bow round her waist and lifted the fabric to her ankles and went faster and faster in circles until the lower part of the dressing gown spun round and round in a circle.

'Ah, Papa this material is so soft and smooth! I love the feel of it. Could I have one like this, in pink?'

'Of course *chérie*, and furthermore, I will make it for you. What do you say to that? Ha?'

She shrieked with excitement, then became motionless, her hand swiftly covering her mouth, eyes shifting from the sofa bed to Leon and back again, because in her exuberance she had forgotten that Leah was still sleeping. To their relief, she hadn't stirred.

'You are kind Papa, I can't wait to get my new dressing gown. I'm off to the bathroom, I'm bursting!' she whispered, hopping up and down while adjusting the safety catch. She rushed out, leaving the door slightly ajar.

The red carpet in the hall and on the stairs led to one of three bathrooms which the tenants were responsible for keeping clean. That included Mr Scott who, sadly, suffered from severe backache. He lived alone in the flatlet next to Leon's, and his rear window looked onto a spacious green lawn whose borders were filled with a multitude of yellow daffodils. Between bluebells, dwarf bulbous crocuses emerged in brilliant yellow and purple.

Whenever Mr Scott bumped into a neighbour, on the landing or in a public place, he greeted them by tilting his trilby towards the middle of his forehead but never actually lifting it off. The gesture was polite and gentlemanly, but his deepest fear was that people might see that he was bald.

Having gone through the formality of smiling and saying hello, his expression would suddenly change. The problem was that you didn't immediately know whether or not he was being serious, for he'd say things such as: 'Did you hear the news? A four-foot man and a nine-foot man have just escaped from jail. The police are looking high and low for them. Shall I tell you about the high wall? I'd better not. You'll never get over it.'

Mr Scott's real name was Schmidt. He had worked most of his adult life in the old-time music-halls as a stand-up comedian, when one day he suddenly decided it might be simpler all round if he were to change his German name by deed-poll to something more English. It now seemed ironic that since then he hadn't had a booking from his agent in over two months.

'I'm at my happiest when I can make people laugh,' he was often heard saying. He liked to stop, in particular, young Mrs Bosch and her husband who were always in a rush, coming and going at all hours of the day and night. He imagined that they missed out on a great deal of fun, so it gave him pleasure when they smiled at his jokes. He wasn't sure whether they really appreciated his humour, but the way he looked at it was that he did more good than harm.

Sylvia had got sidetracked on her way back from the bathroom. Mr Scott switched from telling jokes and went into mime. He used sign language as a form of communication with her. Sylvia took his outstretched hand and happily let him lift her onto the hall table. He then readjusted bits and pieces of his clothing until his appearance was entirely transformed: trouser-legs above his ankles, jacket gathered at the back and pinned together to make a tight fit, sleeves shortened and folded back, his tie a big floppy bow and his trilby punched into the shape of a bowler hat.

The wide staircase with its red carpet is now his 'stage'. He sits on the steps with shoes and socks next to him, nudging bits of fluff from between his toes, feet so highly sensitive that even the slightest touch from his fingers sets him off into bouts of giggling. He quickly pulls a multicoloured blue, green and yellow sock over his foot, only to show an enormous hole. His lower lip quivers, his jaw drops and his eyelids flutter as if they were wings about to fly him away. He stands, lifts one leg round the back of his neck, and rests the heel of his foot on to his shoulder to get a close look at the hole. He has some serious thinking to do! He places one hand on his hip, and with the other scratches the surface of his bowler hat and chin. His shining eyes roll in their sockets, his bushy eyebrows bounce up and down, and his mouth stretches from one side of his cheek to the other while he wags a finger before his face.

He breathes heavily against the knuckles of his clenched fist, rubs them with pride against his chest, turns back the collar of his jacket in slow motion, and produces an invisible needle and thread. In his attempt to get the cotton through the eye of the needle, he holds both so close that they make him go cross-eyed, and then so far away that he can't see the eye of the needle. Finally he succeeds and sews the first stitch, but while pushing the needle through the woollen sock notices that the cotton is much longer than his arm, so he pauses and scratches his bowler hat to think again.

Then with a wink and a nod he rolls back the sleeves of his jacket, bends down, places his shoes on top of the sock as weights, and rushes up the stairs while gently pulling at the cotton from behind. When the hole is mended, he rubs the palms of his hands together and irons the creases in his suit, sits on the stairs and tries to put the sock back on. He tries this way and that way until it dawns on him that he's sewn both ends together. He doubles up laughing, throws the sock over his shoulder, and happily slips his bare feet into his shoes.

He mimicked Charlie Chaplin to perfection (not that Sylvia knew who Charlie Chaplin was until Leon explained that Mr Scott was impersonating the great artist). The expressions and body language so incredibly precise and hilariously funny that he received a standing ovation for what was, for Sylvia, a wonderful performance. Sylvia couldn't remember having ever before laughed so much that her jaws ached. Mr Scott bowed as she went on clapping. With the final bow he disappeared, but promptly returned and presented her with a bunch of daffodils.

9 From Pillar to Post

Leah had had a bad dream and Leon was sitting on the side of the bed trying to console her.

'Someone was screaming at me. They were horrid. I don't know who it was but we were in the cellar. They kept on shouting and getting closer. Their eyes and mouth got bigger and bigger,' she sobbed, 'They frightened me.'

'It's all right, *chérie*, it was only a nasty dream. It's not real! And it's over now. Shall I make you a nice hot chocolate drink...yes...would you like that?' Leon didn't quite know what else he could say or do. Leah's head shook from side to side in a definite NO, and she burst into tears again.

'Yes, it is real! You can't tell me it isn't! I was there. I saw it, and you didn't!' she said adamantly, wiping the mucus from her nose with the sheet.

Leon sighed, exasperated, thinking how like her mother she was in temperament, as if his wife's spirit lived on in Leah. He felt a chill down his spine, and shivered. 'Sylvia, thank God you're back.'

'What happened?'

'She had a nightmare, poor little *shepse*.'[1]

She held the daffodils above her head. 'Look what Mr Scott gave me, aren't they lovely?'

'Yes, they are.' Leon's voice rose with irritation. 'Leah, please stop crying.'

'Papa, it's all right. Here, you take the flowers. I know how to calm her. I had a lot of practice. Remember, I was a Mama to her for years.'

'Yes, yes of course, you must have been. How silly of me not to have realised it for myself. I tried my best, but I can't do or say anything that will comfort her. I heard you outside with

---

1 Dear.

Mr Scott. I was beginning to wonder if one of the neighbours might complain about the noise!'

'Oh Papa, they'll have to get used to it. Little girls cry. Let them complain!'

Sylvia wrapped her arms around Leah and rocked her back and forth while she continued to kiss her face and head. Leon was amazed at how adept and natural Sylvia was in coping with the situation, and how quickly Leah responded. He felt the lack of his ability to do the same, just wanted to close his eyes and sleep. The time on his watch was 11.45 p.m., later than usual, and he hadn't yet finished the hand-stitched button-holes on the jacket. He knew that he would have to work at double the pace the following evening, no matter what else he had to do, if Mr Abramovitch's suit was to be ready by the weekend.

The following morning thick fog and black ice caused havoc on the roads. Dim circular lights shimmered from approaching vehicles in the grey atmosphere. And, as usual, queues outside dress factories in the East End stretched half a mile or more.

The doors opened at 8.30 a.m. and only two people were allowed in at a time. Such a waiting game could take up the best part of the day, with no guarantee of a job at the end of it. As a craftsman at his trade, Leon believed that he would have no problem in getting taken on immediately.

Sylvia and Leah were restless. They were cold and hungry. They had been on the street for almost two hours now, and the queue had hardly moved. 'Papa, I'm so cold and hungry. My legs are freezing. Can we please go?' Sylvia asked.

'Yes Papa, and me, I'm tired too. I want to go back to your house.'

'We will go home soon. First I will go and get us some sandwiches. So just stay here and don't go off anywhere. I will be back quickly.'

'Can we come with you?' Leah asked.

'You'd better stay, otherwise we will lose our place in the queue.' He walked away, and they watched him disappear into the fog.

'How will he find us? He won't see where we are.'

Sylvia tried to reassure herself as well as Leah. 'He will, don't worry.'

'But what if he doesn't? How will we find our way back?'

'I don't know. I suppose we can ask someone to show us.'

'How would this someone know where Papa's house is?' Leah asked, rather puzzled.

The delicatessen was only five minutes away from the factory. Leon knew from experience, having worked in the area before, that the young Jewish couple from Poland, who owned the shop, would have opened for the early morning trade.

Sylvia screamed. 'Oh Papa it's you! Your hand on my arm made me jump. I thought you would be gone much longer. I'm so glad you weren't.'

'Sorry I frightened you *chérie*, but look what I've got for us.'

He opened the brown paper bag and gave them each a hot bagel stuffed with thick slices of *wurst*[1] and, on a separate white piece of paper, a sliced *hamishe*[2] cucumber. A man standing before them in the queue said, ''scuse me mate, don't wish to be rude or nuffink but wouldn't your kids be be'er off at 'ome in the warm like, wiv their mum, given that the wevver's turned so bleedin' foggy and cold? I know my Misses and kids, they won't be steppin' out of doors, not today, that's a dead cert.' He inhaled cigarette smoke deep into his lungs.

Leon was furious, wondering who this man thought he was, criticising him! He looked the stranger in the eye: 'It is none of your concern, why I've got my daughters here with me,' he replied angrily.

'OK guv, keep your 'air on. I only asked. No need to get all bloody stroppy. I ask you, what's this world coming to if you can't 'ave a simple conversation wiv the bloke next ter yer, wivout the likes of you takin bleedin offence at wha I say?'

When Leon finally came to be interviewed he was told by Mr Hyman, the factory boss: 'I would hire you immediately as our floor manager, but it's out of the question until you've made arrangements to have the children off your hands during the day. Come back when you've sorted things out and

---

1 *Wurst* is a kosher salami.
2 A special kind of pickle.

I'll be happy to have you working with us. Pleasure meeting you.'

By the end of the week he'd had more than enough of hearing the same thing, and was worried and anxious, wondering how would he get by and support his family without an income. The small amount he had saved would not last long, and his few private customers didn't provide him with enough work to get by.

His circle of friends consisted mainly of East European Jewish refugees who had fled from Russia, Hungary and Poland, after their families, homes and businesses had been looted and destroyed by the Nazis. Leon had met them either through work or at the Polish club in the West End of London.

Not knowing what to do next, he mentioned the problem to his friends. Many felt sorry for him. Some envied his luck at having found not just one daughter still alive but two, rejoicing at his good fortune. Those who envied him did not do so out of malice, but because it was a painful reminder of their own loss of a son or daughter murdered by the Nazis.

But they were shocked to learn that he had *shlepped*[1] Sylvia and Leah out to the East End factories at six o'clock every morning for the past week. They rallied round with their support, and organised a rota to take turns looking after Sylvia and Leah on the days and nights he went out looking for work.

The girls soon got used to their numerous new Aunts and Uncles, as they became known, with relative ease, such families doing all they could to make sure they had everything needed to make them feel at home. By the end of the second week in England, they only stayed with their father at the weekend.

Leah nevertheless resented the fact that her father had given them up again to be looked after by other people. In the first fortnight she and Sylvia stayed with four separate families, and Leah was unable to accept that these 'Aunts' were trying to take the place of her mother. She was sensitive at taking her clothes off to have a bath, but was not taken seriously by the adults. When she backed away from being kissed on the face, the woman asked: 'What is wrong?'

---

1 Dragged.

'Nothing... really. I just don't like you kissing me.'

'Well, in that case I shan't kiss you again.' She flopped into the chair. 'Is there anything else I do which you don't like?'

'I don't like it when you touch me. And I can even brush my hair myself. Let me show you!'

'No need to bother, I can see that you're a strong-minded child, with a spoilt streak. Shame about that!'

Leah went across the room to place her arms on the clean white ledge of the bay window and watch the world go by. She wondered who the people in the street were. Where were they all going? Where had they come from? Had they a mother and father? 'I wish my Mama was here to look after me,' she said out loud.

There was one couple who Sylvia and Leah loved being with, and they were called Dave and Helen. Both had an abundance of enthusiasm, and a childlike attitude to life that brought fun and laughter to the most ordinary everyday chores.

Helen sang with joy, as a way of keeping her spirits up. She didn't have a particularly good voice or, for that matter, an ear for music, but that didn't dampen her passion for singing. So as she ironed, polished the furniture and the silver, peeled the carrots, parsnips, onions, made *kneidl*[1] for the chicken soup, emptied ash from the fire grate and sewed and baked, she would laugh and often dance in bare feet, pausing every now and then to give Sylvia and Leah a hug and a kiss as they followed her around, copying her every action. They felt love radiating towards them from Helen and Dave, and in return the girls adored them.

'Auntie Helen, I wish I could always live with you,' said Leah watching Helen putting on her make-up. 'Well, just till Mama comes back.'

'*Oy* my little *mensch*, that's such a lovely thing to say. Come here, and let me hug you tight.'

The hug often turned into a tickling session which made Leah and Sylvia laugh till the tears flowed. They were fascinated by all the cosmetics in the drawers.

'Can we put lipstick on, and cream and eye-shadow?' Leah asked, and before Helen could reply, she was dipping her

---

1 A dumpling.

fingers into jars of cream and rubbing it over her face and neck.

'When we come back from shopping, I'll let you both play with the make-up, and I'll even let you dress in my clothes.'

With shrieks of delight, they couldn't wait to get to the shops quickly enough in order to get back and do all those wonderful things.

Helen had escaped from Poland after she had learned that her four-year-old daughter and her husband had been murdered by the Germans. She was in her mid thirties and spoke little English. With her blonde hair and blue eyes she was very attractive.

Dave, her husband, was a Londoner, and both his parents were Jewish. His first wife, incurably ill, had died several years before, and already in his late thirties he had to bring up their teenage son Bertie single-handed. After some difficult and lonely years Bertie, who had grown into a fine young man, had signed on with the Royal Air Force, so was living away from home. Dave had been introduced by a friend to the Polish club, where he met Helen. From then on they saw each other regularly: a courtship which happened effortlessly. He was concerned for her safety because of the long hours she worked, which meant getting back to her digs alone at night, so he would always wait in the foyer of the Odeon Cinema in Leicester Square where she worked the late-night shift as an usherette, selling ice cream and cold drinks. After six months of courtship, in about mid or late 1945, they got married, which was about the time Leon went back to search for Sylvia and Leah in Belgium.

After a long day at work Dave often gave up his evenings to teach arithmetic to Sylvia and the alphabet to Leah. His patience in getting a point across made it enjoyable as well as easier for them to learn. Friends who came to visit would often remark that he was in the wrong profession, but he told them he was happy with what he did. Having started his business from scratch some years ago, manufacturing leather belts and handbags, he was now doing well, and among the luxuries he could afford was a little Austin car, as well as a spacious three-bedroom house in Ladbroke Grove.

On Saturday afternoon everyone sat in the kitchen around the dining table, Dave doing his weekly book-keeping while talking with Leon.

'Leon, the girls, thank God, are wonderful. Believe me, it's a miracle they've turned out the way they have. They're both so sweet. And Sylvia, well I needn't tell you, she has such a good heart, and manners such as I've never seen in a child her age. How old is she, eleven and a half? She's got the mind of an adult, and I guarantee she'll either be a doctor or a solicitor when she grows up. And Leah is Leah – a bundle of energy, a spirit of innocence.'

Leon smiled. 'Strange how different they are.'

'No, not really. Generally siblings are different.'

'Not in my family, we are all very similar.'

'Really! So how are things with you this week, Leon?'

'*Azoy*.¹ Could be better, could be worse. There's this *meschiginer*² woman at work who every five minutes comes over and drives me crazy, she won't leave me alone!'

'What does she want?'

'How should I know?'

'Well, what does she say?'

'She wants me to take her out again.'

'Oh, so you've been having a little romance: well no wonder she's driving you mad. So when did this happen?'

'About a week ago and there is no romance!'

'And . . . ?'

'And nothing. She's not my type.'

'So how come you took her out in the first place?'

'I don't know. You know how it is when they flirt. On top of it she's not a bad-looking woman and very sexy so I thought why not?'

'Where did you go?'

'Nowhere. I took her back to my place.'

'Ah . . . ! I've got the picture.'

'There was nothing in it, it was just a *schtup*³ and now it's become embarrassing.'

'It will pass, don't worry.'

---

1 So so.
2 Mad.
3 Fuck.

'To tell you the truth, there is someone that I like who also works in the same factory. She does the basting there. She came over to England on her own. She can't be more than twenty-six and speaks English like a native. You would never know she was foreign. She doesn't even look Jewish, but she is.'

'So if she's that nice, take her somewhere special, buy her a box of chocolates, some flowers, and treat her like a lady.'

Leon straightened his shoulders against the back of the chair, and tilted his head towards the ceiling as he adjusted his tie. 'Maybe I will.'

'Listen Leon, how would you like it if Helen and I were to look after the girls full-time? Obviously they would be with you at weekends.'

'What? What are you saying! No, I wouldn't want them to live here on a long-term basis. Things are OK the way they are!'

'Well, don't make any decisions now, think about it. I know the girls would be happy and so would we.'

'Look, Uncle Dave, I did the alphabet like you showed me, Look Papa, look.' Leah leaned across the table with the notepad opened in her hand.

'Not now, *chérie*, show it to me later,' Leon said.

Helen handed Sylvia a few side plates and forks from the kitchen cupboard and put more cheese-cake and assorted biscuits on top of what was already there. 'Sylvia, be a little darling and give a plate to everyone. I'm sorry Leon, but I disagree with what you've just said to Dave, and as your friend I have to be honest and frank with you about this. Believe me, we know how difficult the situation is for you and how you're doing all you can, but things are not OK the way they are.'

'What are you talking about?'

'I'll tell you,' Dave said. 'When Helen took the girls to the doctor to be examined this week he told her they have symptoms of malnutrition, but thank God it's only slight, and with a healthy diet they should be all right. He also thinks the girls would be better off living in a family environment that has both parental influences. As for their education, they must start going to a school as soon as possible.'

'What! Can you imagine how I would feel if the girls were to stay here permanently with both of you?'

Dave picked up the notebook Leah had left on the table. 'I would think that you'd be happy for them, what else?'

'Happy for them? So in the future they will consider you as their parents? Are you *meschiger!*[1] he shouted.

'That might be OK for you and the doctor, but it's not OK for me.'

Sylvia clapped her hands over her ears, but not because she didn't want to hear. On the contrary, she would have loved to know what they were talking about but she could no longer remember or understand Yiddish. She also covered her ears because any loud and sudden noise brought on a severe headache.

'Listen Leon, both of them would love to stay here and yes, we'd be more than happy to have them till things improve for you,' Helen said.

'No I don't want to hear any more. I'm taking them back with me now! Come, Sylvia and Leah, get your coats on, we're going home.'

Sylvia kissed Helen and Dave goodbye. 'I hope to see you soon, Auntie and Uncle.'

'Yes *chepse*, please God soon.' Helen replied.

Leah held onto Helen's hand. 'I want to stay here, I don't want to go, Papa.'

'Come on Leah, stop making such a fuss, we're going now!' Leon said, pulling her away from Helen.

'You're hurting my arm, stop it. Auntie Helen, please don't let me go.'

Suddenly everyone stood up and there was a riot in the kitchen, Leah in the middle of a tug-of-war, Leon pulling one way and Helen the other. Dave crouched down, saying to Leah: 'Don't worry, it'll be all right. Helen, if he wants to take them, let him. What's the matter with you, Leon? Why are you acting so crazy? What did we say? We're only trying to do what's best for the children. Is this the thanks we get? Calm down and let's talk.'

'Yes, tell us why you're so upset,' Helen pleaded.

'How can you ask such a stupid question? Just leave me alone!'

'But you mustn't go,' Helen said, 'please, not like this, at least not until we've talked about it calmly.'

---

1 Mad.

Leon didn't reply, and Sylvia, anticipating further argument rushed into the lounge and closed the door so as not to hear them screaming. The evening ended with Sylvia and Leah leaving the house in tears.

10   The Beacon

On our first evening back with father, long after Sylvia and I had gone to bed, I woke to the sound of heavy breathing. The street light shone through the window and curtains. Several feet away from where we shared the sofa bed, I saw Papa's naked body lying on the floor on top of a naked woman. 'What are they doing?' I wondered, closing my eyes and trying to get back to sleep. But curiosity kept me awake, and I peeped above the sheets, eyes half open, hoping Papa wouldn't see me.

I was sexually aroused by their intimacy but, at the same time, felt revulsion and jealous anger because another female was getting Papa's loving cuddles. I saw her get dressed and leave the flat, happy when she had gone, and glad that Papa went to sleep on Sylvia's side of the bed.

We were surprised when, the following day, Papa took us back to Dave and Helen's. I was excited and happy, and so was Sylvia because we stayed for the rest of the week. Papa came on *Erev Shabbat*[1] to take us home for the weekend, announcing over dinner that he had found a wonderful place for Sylvia and me to live.

'I've spent most of the week at the Jewish Board of Guardians, and I can't begin to explain how helpful they have been. They have solved all my problems about what I should do for the best for my girls. The place that they will be going to is known as a Jewish refugee home. Apparently the total number of children that can live there at any one time is sixteen, that's girls and boys together. They will at least be able to mix with other Jewish children of their own age and learn about their cultural heritage, on top of which they will also receive formal education.'

---

1 Friday evening.

'It sounds too good to be true.' Dave said. 'So when is this taking place?'

'They said I can bring the girls on Sunday. What do you say to driving us there?'

'Sure, we'd love to. We're not doing anything, are we Helen?'

'No, and even if we were, we'd cancel it. Of course we're taking you!'

'Do the girls know?' Dave asked.

'I've told them. I think they understand.'

'How often can we visit them?' Helen asked.

'Once a month.'

'Hm, that's not too bad I suppose.' She wiped her eyes. 'I shall miss them terribly. I hope they'll be happy there. And pray that the staff take good care of them.'

'I'm sure everything will be fine,' Leon gave Helen a hug and kissed her on the cheek. 'You know, don't you Dave, that you've got yourself a gem of a woman! You made the right choice, Helen, I would have made your life a misery.'

He certainly would, but four years ago, that was another story. Helen remembered that she would have sacrificed everything to be married to him, and how Leon had refused her proposal, explaining that should his wife Frania be alive, there might be hope for a reconciliation. It confirmed Helen's deepest fears, and she was heartbroken, unable at first to accept the harsh reality that she would only ever be second best. She went on seeing him for several more weeks, but finally plucked up the courage to tell him that she couldn't go on with the relationship. Leon was upset. 'After all,' he said, 'I am very fond of you.'

Helen had spoiled him in every way, so that he considered himself extremely fortunate to have met her when he did. She was, and always would be, someone special to him. Now and again he had toyed with the idea of setting up house with her, but that was as far as he would allow his imagination to run. Now that she had a comfortable life with a good husband in Dave, Leon felt genuinely happy for her, because in his opinion she deserved only the best.

'I thank the good Lord every day for having given me this wonderful man. I love him more than I ever imagined one could love.'

'Helen, you are beauty itself,' Dave said.

Travelling by car was a new experience, and I prayed it would be the last because the trip from London to Tunbridge Wells had me hanging out of the car window, vomiting more times than I care to remember. Dave drove off the main highway into Tea Garden Lane – a long and narrow country road. The pale blue expanse of sky was hidden by a vast canopy of interlaced leaves and buds protruding from the bowed branches. Here, in the midst of the secluded English country-side, was the refugee children's home, The Beacon.

The Victorian building stood on the rise of a hill with panoramic views over acres of woodland, lakes and pastures of grazing sheep. When I got out of the car into the spring sunlight and felt the gentle breeze on my face, the nausea and sickness stopped.

A young woman standing at the entrance to the house greeted us with a warm smile, her bright blue eyes lifting as she greeted father. She wore a light blue blouse and a dark skirt, was about five feet four, with a pale porcelain skin that glowed in the shadowy light. Her face was oval-shaped, with a small full mouth and eyes that seemed to hold some deep wisdom. I noticed her gold wedding ring as she walked gracefully from the porch back into the house, her fair hair glistening in the sunlight which streamed through a window. Sylvia and I followed them, giggling.

'I can tell this is going to be a good place,' Sylvia beamed.

'Is it? I like that lady. I think she's very pretty. Do you think so?'

'Yes. And I've got a feeling she's nice as well.'

Mrs Hirsh led the way into the staff office. 'Please make yourselves comfortable.'

After the refreshments and the formalities, she showed the guests around the establishment.

'What a place!' Dave said: 'And what a location! It must be unique. It's a miniature mansion. Did you see that carving on the oak panelling around the fireplaces? Magnificent! A masterpiece! You can tell it was handmade. And the sheer size of it, from floor to ceiling. A real labour of love.'

'I don't know its history, but I agree it is a beautiful feature of the dining room,' Mrs Hirsh smiled. The spacious room contained a long wooden table, a dozen or so chairs, a sofa, and a piano placed at an angle by the bay window which looked out on to acres of meadows. In the vast living-room next door French windows opened on to a south-facing rock garden, towards a neighbouring farm.

Between the armchairs, toys spilled out of cardboard boxes. Children's books lined shelves on either side of the fireplace, a gramophone and wireless on a lower shelf. Girls and boys of various ages were sprawled on the floor and sofa playing tiddlywinks, dominoes, snakes and ladders, or with plasticine, wooden bricks, jars of water and coloured paints. A train-set was laid out on the wooden floor. Two small girls played cards, calling out 'Snap' at the tops of their voices. They smiled at the visitors, and one of them said: 'You can play with us if you like.'

Sylvia and I were intrigued, seeing most of these games for the first time, and because we could barely understand a word of English, Sylvia asked Uncle Dave to translate what the children were saying.

'Please Miss,' called out a boy of about seven, 'are those two girls coming to stay?' His coal-black hair was thick and curly, his nose and cheeks were covered in freckles. He wore knee-length grey flannel trousers supported by black braces, under a hand-knitted Fair Isle cardigan.

'Yes, Frankie, they're coming to stay,' Mrs Hirsh told him. 'Would you like to introduce yourself?'

'All right! I've been here about a year, and my Mother comes here very often to visit me. I know you'll like it here, it's really good fun. I'm mending a radio – do you want to see it?' He pointed enthusiastically. 'It's just behind the couch!'

'Yes,' said Dave, 'I'd love to.'

A delicious aroma wafted into the living room from behind the wooden hatch in the wall.

'Something smells nice,' Leon commented.

'We have a regular cook,' said Mrs Hirsch. 'She comes in every day from the village. And on Sundays the children eat a traditional English lunch. Either lamb or beef with roast potatoes, Yorkshire pudding and vegetables.'

'It sounds delicious. Is it kosher?' he asked.

'No. But we do light candles on Friday evening for the Sabbath and on holy days, so that the children are kept aware of their Jewish culture.'

'That's wonderful! Isn't it?' Leon smiled at Dave and Helen.

Dave was also delighted, 'This is exactly what they need! The girls know nothing about their own faith. Catholicism is all they've been taught.' He continued talking as they went upstairs from the dining room, back to the main hall and up another flight of stairs. Each of the three main dormitories held six beds: the first for girls between seven and ten, another for the boys and the third on the lower ground floor for girls between eleven and fifteen. Apart from this there was a sickbay, then two single rooms for each of the staff.

'I assure you,' said Mrs Hirsh, 'we will do our best to teach them about Judaism, but the main thing is that they learn to speak English. I'm sure they'll pick it up very quickly, being with other children.'

'You're quite right,' Leon said, 'I'm confident that they'll settle down and do well here. Hopefully, on our first visit we'll hear them speak a little English?'

'I'm sure you will,' Mrs Hirsh smiled.

'By the way, I understand that you work with a colleague, a Mrs Vasser?'

'Yes that's right. Unfortunately it's her day off, but you'll meet her another time.'

'Good, I'll look forward to that. Well, I think that covers everything.' He extended his hand to Mrs Hirsh. 'I suppose we had better make our way back to London now. Thank you for everything.'

'You're welcome to stay for some lunch. The children would enjoy that.'

'That's very kind of you,' said Helen, 'It would be very nice. But maybe we can do it another time.'

'Yes,' said Dave,' that might be better. It's been rather a long and full day as you may appreciate. Besides, it will take us two or three hours to get home.'

'I understand,' said Mrs Hirsh.

'Now remember please, both of you,' Leon said, 'be good girls, and do what you are told. Come now, and give me a big hug.'

'When will you come to see us?' Sylvia asked, as we walked to the main door together.

'We'll be back in four weeks, and that'll seem no time at all!'

Helen said, lightheartedly.

'Bring lots of sweets and biscuits,' I said.

'Lots of them.' Leon held his arms out to indicate the enormous amount.

'Bring the Blue Ribbon biscuits too,' Sylvia shouted after him, as he got into the car.

'I will, *chérie*, don't worry.'

We stood on the porch and waved goodbye. Some time after the car had gone we strolled up and down Tea Garden Lane with Mrs Hirsh, who walked with her arms around our shoulders. After a while, she said, 'Now we'll go inside and join the others, shall we?'

My sister and I were quiet and apprehensive. Several children approached us, but on realising that we couldn't speak English they were amused and laughed, and then lost interest.

'Why have they gone?'

'It's because we don't speak the same language,' Sylvia explained.

On our first night at The Beacon Sylvia and I slept together in the spare room of the attic which, compared to those in the rest of the house, was small, pretty and cosy. Under the sloping ceiling our two beds were separated by a fine yew wood antique cabinet and lamp. Both bedspreads, the lampshade and the curtains, were made of the same cotton fabric: a pale primrose background, covered with bright yellow and blue flowers and shades of green.

On one side of the room, a minute pretty window with thin strips of lead dividing the glass into small diagonal strips, overlooked Tea Garden Lane. The built-in wooden bench below was for storing linen and blankets, and served also as a place to sit, scattered cushions propped against the wall. Embroidered silk tapestries framed under glass hung on various parts of the white walls, while on top of the chest of drawers a vase was filled with blue cornflowers, daffodils, pink heather, tall crimson foxgloves and stems of fern.

We woke in the morning to a chorus of birds and pigeons. Singing and cooing, their melodies were everywhere, in the trees and on the roof, in the bushes and fields.

I remember the moment when I first stepped out on to the flat roof, a blanket of white frost covering the vast open spaces of meadow and forest. The misty atmosphere reminded me of being on the aeroplane flying through clouds and thinking we were in heaven. Here on the roof it felt like that again. Scores of pigeons perched all around the edge of the building, and my only wish was: 'Can I have one, to keep for myself? Please, please ... can I?'

'Well, we can try to get one.'

'Oh, thank you, Sylvia.'

We shivered in our nightdresses and on bare feet crept towards the pigeons, but of course they flapped their wings and flew away. I didn't know whether to laugh or cry, but seconds later they were back. This time we ran in circles trying to surround them, but all our efforts were useless. Back in the bedroom, we were in time to hear the gong strike. One of the older girls came in. 'I think she's telling us to get dressed,' Sylvia said, 'so we can have breakfast before going to school.'

'School?' I shrieked, 'but I can't go there. I don't know anything.'

'You'll learn! That's the idea, *chérie*, in going to school. Hurry, and put your shoes on so I can lace them up.'

Mary, the girl who had come into the room, helped Sylvia and me to get ready. She gently brushed the tangles out of our hair, and neatly tied our ribbons, making sure the bows were round and full and centred on top of our heads. She was about fourteen, tall and slim, light brown hair hanging just below her shoulders, her large hazel eyes sparkling like jewels.

For the first few nights, Sylvia and I shared the attic bedroom, but then we were put into different dormitories, according to our ages.

Rust Hall Primary School was in Tunbridge Wells, about a mile from The Beacon home, and to get there and back we had to walk over the common. Sylvia and I were enrolled on 20 March 1946, but three weeks later I was transferred to the infants' school because, though I was seven, I could neither read nor write – not even my name. Sylvia, however, had had some education before going into the convent, as well as after she had left it.

I sat at the back of the class by the window, day-dreaming,

not understanding anything of what the teacher said. Most of the time I doodled in my exercise book, sketched over and over again the same picture of a desert landscape, with mountains in the distance. In the foreground I drew the figure of a Chinese man dressed in traditional clothes. I liked the picture very much, and remember the feeling of happiness every time I drew it.

I had no idea why this figure always came up, and didn't give it a second thought until many years later when, one day, while sitting with eyes closed doing my spiritual exercises, the picture reappeared in the Seat of Soul located between the two eyes (known as the third eye or the spiritual eye). I was surprised then, but even more so when it was revealed to me that the oriental figure in my childhood drawing had been that of an ancient Chinese spiritual master. During contemplation he had made it known that he understood the deep pain in my life. He realised that in my trouble and confusion I had started to initiate myself into the Secret of Life, and to reach out to God. He told me: 'I have been with you through many of your incarnations, and in this life as well, since you were an infant.' I now understood why the picture I had repeatedly drawn as a child, without knowing the reason, was already familiar to me then. The Divine Spirit had been guiding me home to God.

Two months after our arrival at The Beacon an incident occurred which still haunts me because, to my shame, I was disloyal to the sister I loved so much. On our way home from school one day, Josh, an eleven-year-old boarder and the chief bully at the home, picked a fight with Sylvia. 'What makes you so stuck up, eh? Go on, tell us.' He stepped in front of her, and bellowed abuse right into her face.

'I don't know what you mean. I'm not stuck up. Please, leave me alone.' Sylvia tried to move away, but he went on: 'Hey, where do you think you're going? You haven't answered my question yet. I suppose you think you're better than all of us just because you go around reading books all the time.'

'No. That's not true.'

'Yes it is. Your kid sister isn't stuck up like you. She mucks in with us.'

'Well, I just like to be alone, that's all.'

'That's a load of rubbish! You're just trying to get out of it. I know your sort.'

'Will you please let me pass?'

'Of course.'

He stepped aside and bowed, and as Sylvia walked by he pushed her from behind so that she fell on her knees. 'Stop it. That hurt me.'

'Stop it. That hurt me,' he mimicked. 'Why don't you hit me back. I dare you. Come on. Come on!'

'Please go away!'

'And if I don't? What are you going to do about it?' he sneered. She wept from humiliation, and as the number of onlookers grew, he became more and more aggressive, and pushed Sylvia again till she was lying on the ground.

She didn't notice that the rosary had slipped from under her collar. Josh grabbed it and, with a sudden hard pull, broke the clasp.

I stepped back from the circle of children so as to hide behind them. I didn't know what to do, torn between wanting to help Sylvia yet needing to be accepted by the others. Unhappily, I chose the latter. Josh swung the rosary in the air shouting: 'Look she's a Christian! She's wearing the cross of Jesus!'

There was a murmur from the children, and expressions of shock on their faces. From her crouching position, Sylvia held out her arms and pleaded. 'Please...give it back to me.'

'Here, you want it? You can have it.' With a swift movement he threw it in the air, then he and the group walked away. I followed a few paces behind, leaving Sylvia to search through the grass for her rosary.

The visits from Papa, Helen and Dave made us happy, especially when they brought half a dozen large tins of Blue Ribbon biscuits, chocolates and bags of assorted sweets that were meant to last until they came the following month. I suffered pangs of jealousy and anger whenever Mrs Hirsh distributed the sweets and biscuits among the other children. This was the way things were done, but it didn't make it any easier for me to think it was right.

'Tante Helen, why has Papa come here with Gilda again?' Sylvia asked, 'Who is she?'

'She's your father's friend. He seems very fond of her.'

'Are you?'

'I don't know her well enough to say.'

'Have you noticed that she hardly talks to Leah or me?'

'Sylvia, don't worry your pretty little head about it. Come on, let's enjoy the day. I've been looking forward so much to seeing you.'

'And me. Is she married?'

'Who, Gilda? No. Look, here comes your father.'

It was a beautiful warm summer day as we all sat in the garden together, drinking tea and eating strawberry cream cakes and vanilla ice cream. I proudly showed them how I could ride the battered old bike that all the small children used, and boastfully led them to the tiny patch of garden that Mrs Hirsh had given me. The tomatoes I had planted from seed had thrived, and I ate them with an insatiable appetite. 'You'll turn into a tomato if you eat so many,' Mrs Hirsh teased.

'I like to sit and read over there,' Sylvia pointed, 'under the weeping willow, or the monkey tree.'

'How lovely,' Leon said, 'when I'm in London thinking of you I shall picture you sitting under one of them.'

'O Papa, that'll be nice for you.'

'What other news do you have?'

'I've often asked Leah to sit with me so that I could teach her to read poetry in French. But she isn't interested, she really prefers to run around getting into all sorts of things. But I don't mind Papa.'

'It's not a question of whether you mind, or not. She should listen to you, you're her big sister. No, this isn't good. I'll have to talk with her!'

I charged towards them at full speed on the bike. 'This is such good fun. You should have a go, Sylvia. Oh, I'm so hot and thirsty, can I please have a cold drink?'

'You should come and sit with us for a while, and cool down,' Auntie Helen suggested.

'I will in a minute. Hey Sylvia, have you told them about what happened down at the pond?'

'No, why don't you tell them?'

'Because I'm riding the bike. Anyway you tell it better than me.'

'Two weeks ago when it was very cold and frosty,' Sylvia said, 'a few of us went down to one of the three lakes in the grounds. The water looked frozen, so Leah and some of the younger children, decided to go skating. Then suddenly the ice broke, and they all fell in the water.'

'So what happened?' Dave said, with a serious expression, 'The children shouldn't be allowed on the lakes.'

'They're not supposed to go on it. It was lucky that some of us didn't go on it because we were able to get them out.'

'Thank God you were there,' Leon said, full of alarm. 'They were lucky. Sylvia, you'd better keep an eye on your sister. She's a wild one, not like you.'

'She's all right, Papa. Besides, a couple of the older girls like to look after her. Mary said she wished she was Leah's sister. There's Heather as well, to fuss over her. She's the daughter of the sewing lady who works here. Her name is Mrs Gray but we all call her mum. Every afternoon Heather comes from the school, and while she's waiting for her mother to finish work and take her home, she plays with Leah.'

'Sounds as if our little spitfire is popular,' Leon smiled.

'Well, she is.'

'And, have you got some nice friends too, Sylvia?'

'Not really. But I'm all right Papa.'

'*Chérie*, you must...'

'Papa, please stop it!' She interrupted, 'I'm really OK, I promise.'

'All right *chérie*, if you say so then I won't worry. Shall I read the letter I received from Tante Sara?'

'Yes. What does she say?'

He took the air-mail envelope from the pocket of his jacket hanging on the back of the chair, and carefully unfolded the thin, transparent paper.

'I like that writing,' Sylvia said.

'You do? It's Hebrew,' he replied proudly, 'I can teach you to write in Hebrew.'

'Yes please Papa, I'd like that very much!'

'So the next time I come to visit you I'll give you your first Hebrew lesson. All right. Now, Tante Sara writes that she misses us all very much, so does Uncle Abraham and Charlie, and they would like us to go to Blankenberg and spend the summer together. She wants me to reply soon, and they send all their love.'

'Papa, I don't want to go to Belgium,' Sylvia said.

'Why not, *chérie?*'

'I like it better here.'

'But it would be lovely to go on the beach and swim in the sea.'

'Yes. But not in Belgium.'

'Leon, don't say any more,' Helen said. 'Can't you see she's getting upset?'

'Why should she be upset?' Gilda suddenly asked.

'Do you know what happened to her in Belgium?' Dave asked.

'Only what Leon told me.'

'Then you should understand why she doesn't want to go back,' Dave said. 'Use a little common sense.'

'There's no need to answer her back so rudely,' Leon snapped at him.

I shouted, 'Come and see where I am, Papa.'

A small girl playing close by pointed: 'Leah's up that tree.'

'How could that be?' Helen was surprised. 'She was here just a second ago.'

Leon looked across the orchard to where the young girl was pointing. 'Get down right now,' he shouted, 'do you hear me?'

'Papa, leave her alone.' Sylvia said, 'She's having fun. The children here climb trees all the time.'

I skipped and sang, and came towards them absolutely unaware that there were green and brown stains all over my dress, on my face and hands, and on my legs.

'Look at the mess you've made of yourself!'

'I wanted you to see the tree-house I made. Why didn't you come over?'

'Because I was talking. Anyway it's getting late, and I have to go soon. Besides, I don't like the idea of my daughter climbing trees. That's what boys do. Not girls!'

11 Sylvia

I was asleep in the dormitory with five other girls when Sylvia's voice shook as she whispered my name. 'Leah, Leah, wake up.'

'Why? What's wrong? Why are you in here?'

'I can't see very well. Everything's blurred.'

'Don't be silly, Sylvia, it's night-time. That's why everything's blurred and dark.'

'No, it's not that.'

'What do you mean?'

Sylvia burst into tears. 'I can't see.'

'Don't say that, Sylvia. And please don't cry.' I took her hand and we walked slowly to the bathroom, where I switched on the light. 'That's better, isn't it? You can see now, can't you?'

'No. Everything's a shadow.'

'But why can't you see? Tell me! Let's sit on the floor. What happened?'

'I went to Mrs Vasser and asked for a set of clean sheets because I'd wet the bed again. She was very angry, and told me off for waking her up. She said sleeping on the wet sheets would teach me a lesson. Then she hit me across the head and told me to get back to bed. I felt a terrible pain in my head. As I left the room, she slammed the door, and suddenly I couldn't see anything. My head began thumping inside, and it's still hurting so much...'

'O Sylvia. I'll kiss it better. Wait here, I'll be back in a minute.'

I leapt into Mrs Vasser's room and launched myself onto her bed, and punched her with every ounce of the hatred and pain I felt. 'I'm going to kill you!' I shouted. 'You horrid, wicked thing! What have you done to my sister?' I hit her over and over again, screaming at the top of my voice, 'I'm going to scratch your eyes out!'

Crowds of children appeared, and pulled me off her. Someone took me back to Sylvia, who was lying in my bed, crying. I crawled in beside her just as I had when we were in the convent cellar.

Mrs Hirsh phoned the doctor who, after examining Sylvia, told her to call an ambulance.

The last thing I remember of that night is the doctor giving me an injection to calm me. Next morning Mrs Hirsh informed me that Sylvia had been taken to hospital, and that Papa had come from London to be with her.

The doctor told Papa that Sylvia had a tumour on the brain. The blow across the head from Mrs Vasser had caused the tumour to become more active, and was probably the reason for the sudden partial blindness. It would be possible to operate but the chances of a full recovery were remote, probably less than 50 per cent. Still, there was some hope, so Papa took the decision for Sylvia to be operated on immediately.

When I went to see her three days later, her head was covered in bandages. The operation had not been successful, and she was permanently blind in both eyes.

I sat on the bed holding her hand and talking as if nothing was wrong.

'If Papa stays with that woman Gilda, life will be hell,' Sylvia said. 'But please don't tell anyone I said so. It's our secret. OK?'

'Yes, OK.'

A week later, on 9 September 1946, Sylvia died.

Silently one by one, in
the infinite meadows
of heaven
Blossomed the lovely
stars, the forget-me-nots
of angels.

(Henry Wadsworth Longfellow)

Addendum

In Memory of Sylvia

Fifty-four years ago I had sat under the big monkey tree just as the sun went down, grateful to have passed unnoticed in the crowd of the other children. Pigeons were still perched at the edge of the roof and clouds could be seen through the branches of the tree. I remembered the days I had played in the rural landscape, and Sylvia had sat there with a book. It had been a pleasant time...except for Sylvia. Her unhappiness had been a constant reminder of the past.

Now I was here not with Sylvia but her memory. I sat for a long time, looking at the clouds sailing across the sky. A sudden gust of wind circled overhead, carrying the sweet-scented perfume I recognised – the same sweetscented smell that had filled the cellar with the fragrance of honeysuckle. I thought about how close Sylvia and I had been, and of the many ways God had shown me his gift of love. I had believed in the significance of the radiant faces on the cellar wall, of other planets, of projection from out of the body, of dreams and of the smell of honeysuckle that was there again. I spoke aloud: 'Wind, is it you blowing the honeysuckle scent?'

'Yes,' a voice in the air replied.

'How do you know I like the scent?'

'Because it is written,' the voice told me.

I remembered the time in the cellar when I had sat with Sylvia as she demonstrated what death was: 'You would never see me again if you were dead and I would never see you again if I was dead.' I buried my face in my hands and wept. The stark reality that I would never see my sister again filled me with sadness and remorse. Both for having been unkind to her and for the relief I felt now that she was gone. I looked at the sky and asked her forgiveness.

The other children and staff appeared indifferent to Sylvia's death, and no one talked about her or mentioned her name again. And the shutters went down with a slam.

I went into the house and slept. When I awoke I looked out of the window into the morning light, half expecting to see Sylvia under the tree. A flock of sparrows flew overhead in a V-shape and pigeons nestled on the branches of the monkey tree. It was a sign of Sylvia's presence, I told myself. She was much missed, but it was too late now to tell her.

The traumatic events of my mother's and sister's deaths had lain dormant in me for more than fifty years. In 1993, during a visit to Israel, I had spoken with my Uncle Joel (mother's brother) on the subject of what had happened to my mother – had she ever had a Jewish burial? Later, with help and support from Judith Hassan (director of social services and therapist) at Shalvata, the Holocaust Survivors' Centre – Jewish Care, and Sonny Herman (rabbi) I was encouraged to put my mother and sister to rest. Together with Judith, Sonny and Lyn (my cousin) we went to the cemetery.

Sylvia's grave in the East End of London was unmarked and unidentified. Sonny Herman had my sister's name printed and marked out the grave. A new stone was placed in front of the old one, and the chosen inscription on the stone joined my mother's name with my sister's – Sylvia had always been waiting for our mother to return. We stood at the foot of the grave and Sonny Herman said Kaddish.[1] The symbolism of my mother and sister reunited as 'family' on a gravestone was a painful reminder of my personal losses. Later, a great weight was lifted from my shoulders. This was the moment that the journey of my liberation began. Slowly I re-learned to function and accept life as it is, and came to express joy and love again.

---

1 A prayer.

Appendix

Jewish population in Belgium in 1940: 56,000.

Occupation of Belgium by Nazis: 10 May 1940. Mechelen (Malines), halfway between Brussels and Antwerp, becomes the Centre of Concentration for Deportation of the Jews in Belgium.

Persecution: 14 April 1941: Antwerp pogrom; 27 May 1942: Jews are ordered to wear a yellow star.

Deportation: from 4 August 1941 to 31 July 1944, 25,257 people are deported to Mechelen. Between 1942 and 1944, 28 trains take 25,124 prisoners from Dossin barracks in Mechelen to Auschwitz in Poland. Among them were 5,430 children of whom 150 had not reached their second birthday.

Extermination: 16,000 Jews are murdered on arrival at Auschwitz from Mechelen. Altogether, two thirds of the prisoners were gassed on arrival. Of the remaining third, only 1,207 were still alive when the Nazi camps were liberated.